113

..... TEACH OR PERISH!

INTERNATIONAL BIBLE COLLEGE

TEACH OR PERISH!

An Imperative for Christian Education at the Local Church Level

by

James DeForest Murch

William B. Eerdmans Publishing Company, Grand Rapids, Mich.

Library of Congress catalog card number, 62-11247

First edition, May 1962

Fourth printing, September 1967

PHOTOLITHOPRINTED BY CUSHING - MALLOY, INC.
ANN ARBOR, MICHIGAN, UNITED STATES OF AMERICA
1 9 6 7

PREFACE

In this rapidly changing world, old ideologies, traditions and institutions are giving way to new with such inexorable factuality that we are almost convinced "there is nothing permanent but change."

Many of these changes are for the good of mankind, but there is a tragic tendency to wholesale elimination of the eternal verities and the sure foundations which have made possible the salvation, the welfare and the progress of society.

The forces of truth and righteousness are now facing an Armageddon in which the "spirits of devils working miracles" threaten to destroy them. Humanity's last best hopes are under fire. Christianity and the Church itself are endangered.

Only a few generations in the long history of the world have had the terrible responsibility and glorious opportunity of defending belief against unbelief and the Kingdom of God against the principalities and powers of the Evil One, in times of maximum danger. This is one of those times, and, in the providence of God, it may be the last time.

This volume is written in the hope that in one strategic sector of the Church's life — Christian education at the local church level — a new awareness of importance may be stirred and a new spirit of advance be inspired. Christian education has always been one of the Church's most facile and effective instruments in combating error and in winning and training men for Christ. Unfortunately it is not now measuring up to its tremendous potential.

The times call for some imaginative and challenging proposal which will lift this arm of the Church from the paralysis of tradition and deadly routine into strong and adequate adventure and action. Some years ago the author wrote an elementary treatise, *Christian Education and the Local Church,* which has been greatly used of God as a textbook in many institutions of higher learning. The present volume is not a textbook. It is neither a treatise on the philosophy of Christian education nor a compilation of clever techniques for building "successful Sunday schools." It is a frank evaluation of the present situation in which the Church finds itself; an inventory of its educational potentials; a call for high commitment and zealous action; and a proposal for revitalization, expansion and advance. It is an inspirational, yet practical, appeal called forth by and geared to the times.

The Church and the Church's school have risen to their greatest heights of influence and accomplishment in times of stress and danger. One reason for this is that its mission has taken on greater significance when seen in an enlarged context. The apostolic Church discharged its holy functions in the context of a world lost without the Gospel, the necessity of building the Kingdom of God and the imminence of Christ's return to reign in power and glory. The early Christians were unwithholdingly committed to Christ and no sacrifice was too great for them to make in His service. Something of this enlarged vision and this spirit must grip the Church today and come to motivate its program of Christian education. If this can be accomplished, the world can again be "turned upside down" for righteousness, as it was in the first three centuries of the Christian era.

It is my prayer that this volume, along with many other factors, may be used of God in the accomplishment of His purposes in and through the Church in these crucial times.

—JAMES DeFOREST MURCH

Washington, D. C.

CONTENTS

Chapter I

THIS APOCALYPTICAL WORLD

THE most critical problem that faces the Christian Church today at the local level is its program of Christian Education. In the broad view, it is failing to measure up to the challenge of the times. The Church's paramount need is to become aware of the changed world situation in which it functions. It must then reorient its educational function to the modern cultural situation in such a manner as to achieve more realistically and effectively its God-given purpose.

In some areas of the Christian Church, it is apathetic or antagonistic to the cataclysmic changes taking place and is becoming merely a backwash in the stream of progress. In other words, the Church is making such serious compromises with humanism and secularism that it is in danger of losing its distinctively Christian identity and its ability to exercise a critical, constructive and reconstructive influence in the lives of individuals and society in general. In still other areas the church is faithfully seeking to carry out its Christ-commissioned mission, conscious of the need for revival and new strategies, but hesitant and confused about courses of action.

Christian education is one of the chief functions of the Church. Since its beginnings education has played an indispensably vital role in its welfare and advance. The basic aims, content and

1

techniques of Christian education have remained the same throughout nearly two thousand years but approaches, forms and programs
have changed with changing times. In this crucial period in the
history of the world it is imperative that Christian-education leaders face the situation and take appropriate action. It is the purpose
of this volume to deal with the future of Christian education at
the local church level in the broad perspective of the modern
world situation. This is no inconsiderable or unimportant task.
There are over forty million people now enrolled in church schools
at the local church level in the United States of America. Their
potential in the latter-day apocalpytical conflict between Good and
Evil is tremendous.

What is the shape of our modern world? In this first chapter
we shall begin our kaleidoscopic view with particular attention to
the material world.

Science reigns supreme in the modern world complex. It occu-
pies the same position as the Church occupied in the Middle Ages.
Ever since Einstein said that matter could be converted into energy
and scientists began to do it, mankind has been obsessed with the
idea that science is the source of all that is worthwhile in life.
The material benefits received from science are immense and the
end is not yet. From atomic power to plastic surgery its accomplishments are marvelous — all without benefit of the clergy. The
scientist in his white cassock has largely taken the place of the
black-robed cleric. This new high priest at his best is a man of
integrity who trusts the basic laws of nature to give humankind the
answer to all of life's needs. His loyalty to scientific truth is the
badge of his profession. His capacity for patient and sacrificial
inquiry is limited only by his powers of endurance. His supreme
objective is the welfare of mankind. There are, of course, pseudo-
scientists who do not measure up to this appraisal, but there are
also false priests. Teachers of science are so conscious of their
distinction that they expound their evolutionary doctrine with a
high spirit of evangelistic zeal. They utilize all media of communication to convert the rising generation and to change the
world into their pattern of Utopia.

Naturally there is a keen rivalry between many of the devotees of religion and science. This ought not to be. If scientists would confine themselves to the limits of this material world and religionists would major in moral and spiritual concerns they could happily supplement each other's labors in the quest for Truth. But the stark and realistic fact is that modern culture and mass opinion in general have bypassed religion and have accepted science as the ultimate court of appeal. Even in theology and the humanities certain schools of thought have adopted the "scientific method" to justify their findings and positions. Religious thinking of this nature has become so scientifically objective and frigid that it tends to mummify the feelings, hobble the will and limit its impact on moral and spiritual progress.

The situation is well depicted in the observation of the late Christian F. Gauss of Princeton when he characterized the intelligent man of the Middle Ages as being able to give prompt answers to three crucial questions: (1) What is the purpose of civilization? (2) Where is it going? and (3) Who shall direct it? Medievalists, said Gauss, had no doubt that (1) the salvation of man was its purpose, (2) the Day of Judgment was its destination and (3) the Church and the Emperor would direct it. The intelligent man of this generation is rather certain that science has superseded the Church, but he has no satisfying answers to the other two questions. Indeed, there is an appalling confusion and frustration concerning the ultimate ends of human society.

Ours is a world in which material progress is the chief concern of man. The main theme of conversation is about things and getting things done. In the first six decades of the twentieth century remarkable progress has been made in physics, chemistry, astrophysics, biology, anthropology, archaeology and all the physical sciences. The atom has been smashed and harnessed. The Antarctic and the Arctic have been explored. The moon and the planets are about to be occupied. Commerce has pyramided its corporate strength and millionaires are almost "a dime a dozen." Gadgets of every description have taken the slavery out of work and automation bids fair to eliminate physical labor altogether. Scientific medicine has added ten years to human life expectancy and is winning the battle to eliminate polio, cancer and all forms of bodily disease. Great dams and irrigation projects and the discovery of ways to purify sea water have made possible the productivity of the world's arid lands. Redistribution of populations and food surpluses are among the grandiose plans to eliminate starvation and provide universal prosperity. Construction of skyscrapers, public buildings and monuments, cultural centers, industrial and commercial complexes and communication facilities have outdistanced all similar achievements in human history. What a contrast to the days when the temple and cathedral dominated the landscape and awed the common man. Small wonder that men, who measure things in terms of the five senses, question the relevance of religion to modern life.

This is a world of ever widening horizons. Distance has been annihilated and time is beginning to lose its meaning. In America men have seen the stagecoach give way to the railroad, the railroad to the automobile, and the automobile to the airplane. The other day two men headed east from Los Angeles, one by train and the other by air. When one landed in Paris, the other had only reached Elko, Nevada. This is typical of today, but what of tomorrow? Rocket travel will soon make transportation to all parts of the world a mere matter of minutes instead of hours and days. When world-wide satellite communications are perfected man can talk by radio and see by television as well as telephone from any point on earth to any other in all kinds of weather and under any atmospheric condition. With the help of navigation satellites, man, as he rides, sails, flies or walks over the earth will know exactly where he is at any time. The shipper, the farmer, the golfer and the flier will know what to expect weatherwise, through improved metereological satellites. Dr. Wernher von Braun has observed that "in these days of mushrooming technologies nobody can know exactly what kinds of amazing developments we shall see, nor how they will affect men's lives. We can only be sure that we will continue to be surprised beyond measure."

Man used to construct little isolated kingdoms of his own in which he ruled with solitary authority, but today all such walls have been or are being penetrated. The relative peace and contentment of Welcome, Maryland, or Fly, Kentucky, have been disturbed by concern for Kuwait, Kashmir and Katanga. The familiar and safe universe which men once left to God is now the subject of scientific exploration or political controversy. The moon, Mars, Venus and Saturn are only as remote as the departure of the next rocket. Lebanon, Arabia, Egypt and Israel, which were once mystical Bible names, are now in the headlines of the daily papers with their political eruptions threatening the peace of the world. There is scarcely a foot of the earth's surface or a sector of human society that has not been photographed and piped into our living rooms by television. Our sudden projection into a universe of overwhelming power, amazing new knowledge, incredible speeds and vast distances has collapsed yesterday's world, and things will never be the same again. Unless the Bible and the Christian religion are taught with a new relevance to man in this new broad-horizoned age, they will not be considered worthy of a hearing.

Space-age sophisticates are, however, not without their moments of sober reflection concerning their achievements. For example, they wonder whether a world-wide television and communication system might not be used by unprincipled men to mend and twist the wills of whole peoples for the accomplishment of evil ends. They concede that half-truths and lies could be broadcast in such a clever and convincing manner as to deceive the very elect. They realize that certain great totalitarian nations are likely to utilize such means to gain control over the most impressionable areas of the globe and destroy our own freedoms.

This is a world in which the individual is increasingly under death sentence by cold, hard organizational complexes designed to achieve social ends. "Personal rights," "individual freedom," "free enterprise" and other such concepts are becoming *passé*. In America, the welfare state, governmental bureaucracy and sociological controls; in the world, the United Nations, UNESCO, WHO, ILO, et cetera are binding mankind with the thongs of organizational conformity. DeTocqueville once prophesied that if America is ever destroyed it would be "by intensifying the social virtues at the expense of others, by making the individual regard himself as a hostage to prevailing opinion, by creating, in sum, a tyranny of the majority." The new social dogma holds that the group is the source of creativity, that the individual must be tightly integrated in organizational units, that everyone must be democratically directed in the achievement of common desirable and benevolent goals. This doctrine in practice undermines individual courage to express views opposed to group opinion. Mankind is slowly being resolved into a faceless society under an organized tyranny more subtle and persuasive than any democracy ever sought to destroy. But thinking men are restive under such controls and like William H. Whyte, Jr., in *The Organization Man*, are seeking release. Christianity with its emphasis on the dignity of man and his individual horizontal relationship and responsibility to God holds the ultimate answer in this quest.

This is a world torn by revolution. Explosive political and social upheavals are occurring all over the globe. As this paragraph is written, Asia, Africa and Latin America are especially crucial areas. The "have-nots" are demanding their share of material prosperity hitherto held and controlled by propertied aristocrats and bourgeois. The masses in the ghettos of the great cities, the jungles and remote villages of the interior are realizing that their day is here and revolution can bring them a new life beyond mere existence. In the well-established democracies, like the United States of America, old patterns are under fire in every area of life. The hopes, the dreams, the aspirations of the underprivileged clamor for realization. Demands for racial equality alone threaten social upheaval unprecedented in the history of the world. Where is the moral and spiritual leadership comparable to that of Moses or Paul to guide the masses toward the achievement of their highest good? What word has the Church above and beyond the welter of clashing self-interest and group hatreds, which can bring peace and goodwill among men?

With repudiation of old authorities and rejection of old *mores* comes a veritable "confusion of tongues" similar to that which took place at the ancient Tower of Babel. Strange philosophies and ideologies are hailed only to be rejected. Rival claims of social, economic and political leaders incite cold wars. In religion, long quiescent faiths now rise again to contend for the minds and hearts of the masses. Even Christianity itself is fragmented into hundreds of denominations, sects and cults unable to present a united front against the common enemies of Christ. Name any field of human endeavor and the same disorder and confusion will be found. Can men any longer find unity in Christ?

Like the men at Babel, our modern world, claiming to be wiser than God, finds release in animal passions. A sensationalist personal and social ethic encourages man to measure his experience in physical correlates. It assumes uniformity between man and nature and eschews all moral and spiritual restraints. A beatnik generation practices sex anarchy without a twinge of conscience. There is a rapid increase in pre-marital and extra-marital sex relations, homosexuality and other sex deviation, and a multiplication of rapes, divorces and prostitution. Frank pornography and obscenity mark this horrible subversion of the sensate order and find expression in music, painting, sculpture, the press, the theater, moving pictures, television and all forms of cultural life. George Sokolsky, popular newspaper columnist, observes that modern music reflects this beatnik spirit in its retreat from harmony to noise. Schumann, Beethoven, Bach and Mozart give way to drum choruses, imitations of street and factory noises, and the jazz concoctions of Basin Street and the African jungle. As long as this crumbling of the moral order continues and no new and better structure is built, there is a grave threat of the eventual loss of all moral values. Pitirim A. Sorokin of Harvard warns that if a third world war should come in the midst of such a demoralized society there would be a reversion to bestiality the like of which humanity has not seen for centuries.

Yet this is a world which yearns for Utopia. Communism, seeking an alliance with science, and basing its promises on an enlightened materialism, is offering humanity a classless paradise.

All sources of natural wealth, they say, will be available for the full-orbed development of mankind through continuous growth and progress in science and technology. This, promise Red leaders, will be guaranteed by governmental implementation of the great socialistic principle, "from each according to his ability, to each according to his needs." Everyone will live in easy circumstances. Collective and state farms will produce an abundance of food and other necessities of life without cost to the consumer. There will be well-appointed housing free of charge. Hard physical labor will disappear. There will be plenty of social and cultural benefits for all. Public wealth will be distributed among all members of society, irrespective of the quality or quantity of their work. There will be free education, free institutions, free use of public amenities, free medical care, pensions, provision for child care and a peaceful existence without threat of war or destruction. Communism has not yet been able to deliver, but the bait is enticing. Something approaching this idyllic state is promised by social-welfare specialists in the free democracies.

But Utopian dreams are rudely marred by the shadow of universal nuclear destruction. General Curtis LeMay was quoted not long ago in *The Washington Post* as saying that "a nuclear war is inevitable" unless nations respect their agreements and desist from aggression. If such a war were to come, the great military leader is reported as saying it could begin and end in thirty days. In that interval every major city in America — Washington, New York, Philadelphia, Detroit, Chicago, Los Angeles — would be reduced to rubble. Similarly the major cities of all enemy lands would be utterly destroyed. Less than one-third of the world's population would survive. Is this the world that scientists and materialists have given us? There are few men who dare to speak with such frankness and honesty. The fatalism and futility which fill men's hearts with fear are usually hidden under false optimism and smiles which pass in the night.

New Testament Christianity is surprisingly relevant to this apocalyptical world. Even the most worldly-minded can see that the Apostle Peter "makes sense" when he prophesies a "Day of the Lord" in which "the heavens shall pass away with a great noise" and "the elements shall melt with a fervent heat, the earth also and the works that are therein shall be burned up." It could actually happen in dreadful nuclear reality. Moderns can find reality in John's vision on the Isle of Patmos in which he described the end of civilization: "Babylon the great is fallen, is fallen, and is become the habitation of devils, and the hold of every foul spirit, and the cage of every unclean and hateful bird." These are indeed times in which mankind is witnessing a basic struggle between Good and Evil, between the Christ and the Anti-Christ.

But there is a brighter side to any balanced appraisal of the modern world. God is still in His heaven. His promises are forever sure. Christ, the living Christ, is still the world's hope. The "gates of hell" shall not prevail against the Christian Church. There are still multiplied millions of Christians who have not "bowed the knee to Baal" and who constitute a mighty potential for the mounting of a new Christian offensive.

It would also be erroneous to assume, because of the shattering changes from the old order to the new, that the remaining worthy values of our Western culture are insignificant. Our civilization, if spared nuclear destruction, may persist as a mighty force in the affairs of men for hundreds of years. History reveals that the Hittite, Babylonian, Egyptian, Hellenistic and Roman cultures were centuries in disappearing even after the seal of doom was placed upon them. Christianity had some of its finest years, difficult as they were, when it rose Phoenixlike out of the ashes of a dying Rome. While Christianity and Western culture should not be thought to be identical, the Church should not declare war against a society which it has had such a large part in creating. Its highest and best values were derived from the Bible. There are significant movements within it which are motivated by Christian idealism and are in harmony with the spirit of the Christian Gospel. That which is good is honored by the whole world and is widely influential in the institutions which form such a vital part of modern life. While condemning the evils and warning against the dangers implicit in Western civilization, the Church may well join hands with all its forces which seek the highest good of and for mankind. Many of the products of inventive genius and the investigations of pure science are contributions to spiritual as well as material progress. The effectiveness of the Church's mission is enhanced by the printing press, the radio and television. Reverent scientists assure us that there will be still further discoveries which can be media for disseminating the Gospel and winning souls to Christ. The God-given powers of the mind were intended to be exercised in the natural world as well as the spiritual. The Church should rejoice that it can have a part in teaching the liberal arts and sciences, in creating and maintaining an atmosphere conducive to material progress. It should be proud to have a place as an ameliorating influence in the culture of which it is a part. As J. Gresham Machen put it in *Christianity and Culture*, "Instead of destroying the arts and the sciences or being indifferent to them, let us cultivate them with all the enthusiasm of the veriest humanist, but at the same time consecrate them to the service of God. Instead of stifling the pleasures afforded by the acquisition of knowledge or by appreciation of what is beautiful, let us accept these pleasures as the gift of the Heavenly Father. Instead of obliterating the distinction between the Kingdom and the world, or on the other hand withdrawing from the world into a sort of intellectual monasticism, let us go forth joyfully and enthusiastically to make the world subject to God."

These apocalyptical times present the Church with an unprecedented opportunity and challenge. This is no time for Christians to get an otherworldly look in their eyes, to counsel monastic isolation from reality. It should be a time of evaluation of the situation in which it finds itself, of introspection and repentance, of rededication and reorientation, and of advance under God as an army mighty with banners. The Church, like the seven churches in the Apocalypse, is already under divine evaluation and faces the judgment of Almighty God. Will it measure up to the divine standard?

Chapter II

IS THE CHRISTIAN ERA ENDING?

THE vast expansion and influence of Christianity has been one of the amazing phenomena of history. Nearly two thousand years since its founding, it is still the most powerful force for righteousness in the world.

During the last 150 years of its existence it has had its greatest geographical extension and its widest influence on mankind. And yet, serious observers and thinkers within and without the Christian Church are saying, "Christianity is in retreat; the Christian era is ending."

This is not the first time the prophets of doom have sounded the death knell of Christianity, but it must be conceded that the forces which now oppose it are more subtle and powerful than any it has ever faced. History reveals that this Faith has moved forward by major pulsations alternated by serious recessions. Hitherto, each advance has carried it farther than the one before. Is the current recession but one in the series, to be followed with Christianity's greatest surge in history? Or is this the beginning of continuing regression?

Unfortunately Christianity is often equated with Western culture and confused with it. So great has been the influence of the Church in human affairs that nations which hold it in highest regard are often called "Christian nations." Where these nations have maintained an extensive colonial system and favored Christian missionary activity, the rising tide of nationalism and revolution is destroying the political system and threatening the Faith as well. The pagan religions, in this changed atmosphere, are showing new life, reassessing their insights and making high claims of superiority. In a growing number of areas they are asserting their power and demanding that doors hitherto open to the preaching of the Gospel be closed.

In India, leading thinkers in Hinduism now claim that their religion is the true basis of all religion. The noted Radhakrishnan, Vice President of India and long an outstanding Hindu philosopher, says Hinduism is not only a religion but expresses all religion in its most universal and profound terms. Laws repressive of Christianity have been passed and it is predicted in some quarters that in five years there will be no more Christian missionaries in India. This is but one typical example of many such situations around the world.

International Communism, grounded in an atheistic Marxian materialism, and sweeping the world like a holocaust, is Christianity's bitterest enemy. Communist leaders recognize Christianity as the chief barrier to their conquest of the globe. Russia, the world center of Communism, while claiming to guarantee religious liberty, has ruthlessly slaughtered millions of Christians and permits no evangelistic or educational effort by the churches remaining within its borders. Communists have fought and filtered their way into many lands until their godless system dominates over one-third of the human race. No setback to Christianity in recent times has been more grievous than the expulsion of the Christian mission to China. Though China has never been free from turbulence, Christianity survived the Boxer rebellion, the overthrow of the Manchu dynasty and the Japanese invasion. Then, as its influence was rising and reforms were being effected, Communism cut off missionary bases, closed churches, took over educational and charitable institutions, executed thousands of Christians and cruelly tortured and exterminated all Christian missionaries. Where Christianity has been so strong that Communist governments feared openly to challenge it, slow, subtle but certain means of elimination are being applied, as in Poland and East Germany. The Red Anti-Christ will not be satisfied until the last vestiges of the Faith in the earth are completely destroyed.

In lands where the Church is the ward of the State, as in England, Sweden, Denmark, Spain and the Latin American republics, a pall of nominalism hangs over the Christian population. Numbering hundreds of millions, there is among them little sense of the moral and spiritual relevance of Christianity to the individual or to society. The magnificent church buildings, which rise like great monuments to the dead, are seldom filled with worshippers even on holy days or festivals. Millions never go inside except for christenings, marriages or funerals. This indifferentism is probably the chief weakness of Christianity as it faces the modern crisis.

It is, however, not within the purview of this chapter to deal extensively with the world situation. Our primary concern is within the narrower context of American Protestantism. Here it is widely conceded that America is now in a definitely post-Protestant era.

America has long been the proudest example of full-flowered Christianity. It was founded by Puritan gentlemen, Cicilian peasants, Irish potato diggers and political refugees, Dutch fishermen, German and French intellectuals and mechanics — pioneers on new frontiers of freedom. The Puritans, who came seeking the right to worship God according to the dictates of conscience, exerted the strongest moral and spiritual influence in the making of America. They shaped much of the influential social and political framework of the new nation. Timothy Dwight's epic poem, "The Conquest of Canaan," describes them as building a nation under God, in a mood reminiscent of the Old Testament history of Israel. America came to represent freedom under God. Tides of immigration brought thousands who yearned to think and act as free men. The Declaration of Independence breathed that spirit. Men were affirmed to be born equal with all the attributes of human dignity and the God-given right to life, liberty and the pursuit of happiness. There were social stratas in the new land but they were not allowed to fossilize into caste barriers. Every man had a right to his own opinion, right or wrong, and to express it and propagate it. As the republic took shape, these freedoms were preserved and guaranteed by the Constitution of the United States. The God-centered ideal persisted for two hundred years, shaping a new society which became the envy of all nations. This ideal is far from dead today, but it is in grave danger of being eclipsed and lost if current trends are not halted and the Christian ethic is not rebuilt into the minds and hearts of its citizenry.

America became through the years an essentially Protestant Christian nation. With the Revolution of 1776 the ties with old-world totalitarian religion were broken. With separation of Church and State and freedom to read the Bible and interpret, it, over 250 denominations and sects developed. Roman Catholicism and Judaism came to thrive under the same freedoms enjoyed by Protestants. But Protestantism still maintained its numerical ascendancy and its strong influence in social and political affairs.

Institutionally it would appear that American Protestantism is flourishing today. It has more members than ever before. It has billions of dollars worth of church buildings and is enjoying a construction boom in which chapels are being replaced by sanctuaries, and sanctuaries by edifices of cathedral proportions. It has other billions in endowments and permanent funds. It controls, supports or maintains connections with over five hundred colleges and universities. Protestant presses publish thousands of books and brochures each year and magazines with circulations high in the millions. Its charitable institutions are numbered in the thousands and its life-insurance and annuity systems have assets in the billions. Protestantism is "big business" and it is "run" by thousands of capable clergymen and ecclesiastical executives.

But there are signs of serious weakness, even impotence, in this vast structure. This fact is the subject of wide discussion — almost a public scandal. The Right Reverend James A. Pike, Episcopal Bishop of California, is saying that Protestant retreat is evident on every hand. Dr. Will Herberg of Drew, one of the shrewdest critics of religion in America, says Protestantism no longer deeply affects the lives of people. William H. Whyte, Jr., in *The Organization Man*, says the "Protestant ethic" no longer seems to have pragmatic value in modern society. Roman Catholic critics, like Father Thurston Davis, editor of the Jesuit magazine *America*, says the nation has "virtually ceased to be Protestant." Since a Roman Catholic has been elected President, there are many Protestants who would agree with that view.

What are some of these disconcerting signs of decay in American Protestantism?

Foremost is the appalling ignorance of most Protestants concerning religion. They are for the most part highly intelligent about other things, but they are religious morons. They have been brought up in homes where parents seldom discuss religion and feel no obligation to give religious instruction. They send their children to secular schools where religion is too often studiously avoided and sometimes treated with sophisticated disdain. The churches largely lack a comprehensive educational program which instructs in basic Christian facts and doctrines. There are Bibles galore in living rooms, bedrooms, purses and libraries, but they are seldom read. When they are, it is for sentimental reasons and without understanding. Ask the average Protestant why he is a Christian, or a Protestant, or a Methodist or whatnot, and he can seldom give an intelligent or valid answer.

Coupled with their ignorance of basic Christian doctrine and denominational distinctives is, what Russell Kirk called, in *Fortune* magazine, "complacency and Pelagianism." Pelagius, a fifth-century heretical theologian, taught that there was no original sin, that man was endowed with natural goodness, should work out his own salvation and that God's grace is sufficient. These modern Pelagians out-Pelagius Pelagius. He preached and taught with burning conviction the necessity of active personal faith and of growth in grace and the knowledge of the truth. Too many modern Protestants are unconcerned about Christian doctrine and think that happiness may be achieved by togetherness, goodwill, adjustment to things as they are, and improving their social status in the community.

Clair Cox in *The New-time Religion* frankly charges that the modern Protestant church has "joined the world." Half the members stay away from church services because of the house, the automobile or the boat. To attract people, church leaders have to provide more and more recreational facilities and club rooms. The church doors are open twenty-four hours a day for steak dinners, coffee and cocktail hours, smokers, swimming, skating, bowling, ping-pong, shuffle-board, bridge and bingo. Church edifices themselves reflect the trend and may well be mistaken for silos, tepees or glorified barns. There are even theater shells and bandstands on church property, devoted to the production of drama, spectacles and festivals. The tithe and sacrificial stewardship are replaced by raffles, bazaars and rummage sales for church financing. When funds are needed for building projects and other major undertakings the church calls on "the best brains in the world of the bulls and the bears." In this process of change from the old- to the new-time religion, churches are becoming so alike that the clergy as well as the parishioners find it easy to jump denominational fences and go wherever the pastures are greenest. People join the church for much the same reasons they join a club. Vance Packard in *The Status Seekers* suggests that church membership gives Americans a certain social status. It imparts a false show of piety and business ethics and affords easy psychological adjustment. It is a good thing to indicate when making application for a job. The children of these people are *sent* to Sunday school, but because of their home background they give only empty responses to the symbols of religion. Many of them turn out to be juvenile delinquents. Recent surveys in large cities, according to Dr. Milton J. E. Senn, showed that three-fourths of their delinquents attended church or Sunday school and came from homes where parents were church members.

In such a climate there is, of course, theological chaos. For the past half-century there has been a devastating war between "liberals" and "evangelicals." The latter insist that "the Bible is the religion of Protestants" and that the historic evangelical Christian faith must be kept inviolate. Liberals, highly critical of the Scriptures, reject much of the Old Testament as myth and barbarism and the New Testament as superstition and antiquated ethics. There are signs of theological revival but the voices are confused. The average minister and the few laymen who care are perplexed and bewildered by the conflicting ideas of Barth, Brunner, Kierkegaard, Niebuhr, Tillich, Bultmann, Troeltsch, Calvin and Arminius. Before the "war," Christian doctrine was dispensed in simple terms in catechisms and Bible memory verses and was accepted as God's revealed truth. Now there is little or no agreement about what ought to be believed.

Disillusioned about Bible truth and traditional theology, many Protestant leaders have turned to a "social gospel." This nineteenth-century movement, initiated by Walter Rauschenbusch and his colleagues, sought to apply the social ethic of the Christian Gospel to the evils of modern industrial society and to bring about drastic social revolution. Christ's Kingdom, they said, must be realized on earth through the social and political reconstruction of society. A recent report of the Lilly Endowment, one of the few big foundations interested in Protestantism, says, "The passion born of the social gospel, so much in the foreground a generation ago, has now worn quite thin. . . . Man is seeking something more than bread and erudition." Latter-day "social gospelers" find their chief satisfaction of soul in "sit-ins" to promote integration of the races, fighting rent gougers, lobbying for social-welfare legislation, slumming, statistic gathering and tinkering with problems of abnormal psychology.

Sometimes Protestant frustration leads to a species of escapism which takes refuge in a new emphasis on symbol and liturgy in worship. As the Spirit departs from the Church there are desperate efforts to recapture it in forms and ceremonies. There is a rash of articles, editorials and books on ritual, rubrics, litany and mystical rites for Protestant churches that formerly avoided religious formularies as "works of the devil." Theories of transcend-

ence are being spun to lift the human spirit and give men a new
"peace of mind" and "optimism" through worship. Satisfying worship services amid highly cultural surroundings which cause people
to forget the realities of life are often the chief concern of the
clergy.

Alongside worship as a tranquilizer may be placed the new emphasis on Christian psychology. Religion is being offered as a
nostrum to bring peace of mind and domestic tranquillity. The insights of depth psychology undoubtedly offer worthwhile values
and standards, but these are no match for the biblical Christian
principles of eternal security and moral responsibility.

There is no use blinking the deleterious effect of sectarian divisions upon American Protestantism. Possibly there have been
some values in competitive religion but it is increasingly apparent
that these crisis times demand not only a united Christian front
but the integrated total resources of the Church if it is to overcome
its enemies and achieve its God-given goals. Much energy is
wasted in maintaining separate and often duplicate organizations
and underlining differences which may have had some meaning
in the past but are now largely irrelevant to the well-being of the
body of Christ. Men find it hard to believe in a fragmented
Christ and a warring Church. To correct this situation there is a
growing ecumenical movement which is promoting mergers of
"church families" and integrating church functions in councils of
churches, but many of these efforts are concerned with little more
than institutional reorganization and ecclesiastical strategy. They
may well succeed and the resultant united church be but a sar-
cophagus for a dead faith.

This is admittedly only one side of the whole picture of American Protestantism. A further and more optimistic word will be
spoken in a later chapter, but this description is sufficiently factual
to cause thinking men to see through the veneer of Protestant
"success" the weaknesses and failures which call for prayer, repentance, renewal and advance.

This study would not be complete without a look at the American culture which has been so proudly called "Christian." It is

undoubtedly true that Protestantism as a strong, uncompromising, aggressive moral and spiritual force has dominated American life. The late Albert Jay Nock once said that the United States at one time had a virtual "established church." It was not a matter of law but of sheer moral influence exercised by a majority of the population which was Protestant. The government was run by Protestants or politicians who knew that their success depended on conformity to what has been called "the Protestant ethic." Business was run on Protestant moral principles. The public schools were controlled by Protestant school boards, superintendents, principals and teachers who accepted and taught Protestant moral ideals. Practically every sector of American life bowed to this Protestant ethic.

What was this ethic?

It was based on a universal belief in the sovereignty of God, the divinely revealed law of God, the God-given freedom of the individual and the overruling direction of Divine Providence. Coupled with this was the conviction that by God's help any worthy ambition was within the range of achievement. For over three hundred years America was a land of open opportunity. Wide stretches of territory and great natural resources were unclaimed. Beyond new horizons and new frontiers lay hope of riches and a new life. Nothing could "keep a good man down." In this climate God-centered persons prospered and material progress was greater with each succeeding year.

In the "game of life" there were certain accepted rules. They began by taking God into account. His moral code must be obeyed. Respectability included going to church on Sunday and engaging in no worldly pleasures or business on God's day. Most leaders of community life had high regard for the clergy, paid their church dues, read their Bibles at least occasionally, prayed and did a little church work. Prayer before a business deal was not an uncommon practice. All the blessings of life were considered the gift of God. A rich man was considered a special mark of God's favor. There was even a Thanksgiving Day each year in which the whole community assembled in some church or churches to thank God for its material growth and prosperity.

Then, there was hard work. Slothfulness was considered a sin. It was believed that genius was at least half due to a full day's work. Self-denying workers seldom looked at the clock and were willing to labor sixteen hours a day if that were necessary to achieve a worthy goal.

Honor and integrity were prized possessions. It was believed that shrewdness and ambition were good but not the sacrifice of virtue. "A man's word was as good as his bond." The friend dependable and true, the advisor honest and fearless, the competitor just and chivalrous were characteristic of American business at its best.

Freedom of the individual and his God-given constitutional rights were either respected or demanded. Individuals were free to earn a living and climb their ladders of success in their own way. They could choose their own professions or change them at will. They could exercise their genius for making or managing money in any lawful way. If by dint of superior skill or intelligence a man chose to live better than his neighbor he could do so and his neighbor was free to excel him if he could.

Merit was the best qualification for advancement and success. Whether in men who were poor, underprivileged or unknown, or wealthy, cultured and socially fortunate, merit was recognized for what it was and usually rewarded.

Thrift was the hallmark of all worthy men. As soon as a young man began to earn money he began to save a portion of it. It was considered a good rule to put away a dollar out of every ten earned. Even the schools taught the habit and each child had his own savings account. It was believed that at some point in life these accumulated savings might either be the nucleus for starting a business or making a rewarding investment, or providing an "umbrella for a rainy day."

This so-called "Protestant ethic" reached out beyond the business and industrial life of the nation. It was responsible for the emancipation of the slaves during the Civil War of 1861-65. The state papers of President Abraham Lincoln during that dread period of our national history often read like pages out of the Bible. During the "Golden Age of the Sunday School" (1900-1916) moral right instead of political expediency often determined elections and motivated such movements as woman's suffrage and prohibition of the manufacture and sale of alcoholic beverages. The Protestant ethic called for humility and repentance when America was known to be in the wrong, for solving problems of ignorance, disease and poverty, for helping the "little people," the hungry, the helpless, the homeless, the friendless and the oppressed.

But with the growth of the nation into a major world power, life became more and more complex. Dilemmas were faced which began to test the validity and the adequacy of its moral and spiritual principles. The empire builders, the great tycoons, the prosperous workers and the wielders of great power came to identify "the American way of life" with material prosperity. The whole nation, proud of its achievements, began to talk big, act big and grow big. Then came business mergers, consolidations, mass production, capitalistic imperialism, corporate labor, governmental bureaucracy and highly developed societal organization. Material prosperity created a secular spirit. People became more interested in new cars, sleek boats and week-end larks than in God's day or, for that matter, God Himself. After all, what could God do for a man whose every move was regulated by some company, corporation, union, government bureau or social organization?

In the ensuing fight for survival, the ethics of the jungle were revived. Lying, double-dealing, cheating, stealing and the like were camouflaged with an uncertain respectability and condoned if they achieved success and brought material prosperity. The pragmatic values of honor, integrity, thrift, hard work and individual freedom came into serious question. The Church seemed no longer very relevant to the hard facts of life.

Public education, from the elementary schools up through the universities, began to bypass religion. It turned from the God-centered ideas of America's founding fathers to a philosophy of secular naturalism and scientism. It began to find its goals in the adjustment of its pupil to the changing order. It ceased to concern itself with the deep issues of man's purpose and destiny. Its attitude toward the conflicting philosophies of the public forum was marked by objectivism and neutralism. While professing a high standard of ethical idealism, it turned away from a divine source of a fixed moral code, to the changing mores of a pluralistic society. This abandonment of the old Protestant ethic has contributed to what Dr. John A. Mackay calls "the pervasive sense of emptiness that marks our modern culture." Charles Peguy calls the man who is the product of such an education, a "monster of uneasiness" and the easy victim of all sorts of subversive doctrines and movements.

From these observations and for many other reasons which might be adduced in a comprehensive study, it may well be concluded that America is not only in a "post-Protestant era" but that Western civilization is entering what Arnold Toynbee calls a "post-Christian era." This is not to say that the Christian Gospel itself is less vital and dynamic than it was in the first three centuries of its existence. It is still the power of God unto salvation to the individual and thereby the hope of human society. But that dynamic is not being released through the instrumentalities of the modern Church with the all-pervading and inextinguishable flame that is essential if the gathering gloom of the world is to be dispelled.

Chapter III

CONFUSION OF TONGUES

HAVING left the sure path, the main road by which the high achievements of the race have been attained, man is like a wanderer "tossed to and fro, and carried about with every wind of doctrine, by the sleight of men, and cunning craftiness."

The nation having abandoned its "Protestant ethic" is losing its sense of purpose, its serious convictions, its moral code, its hard discipline and its willingness to sacrifice for a holy cause. It no longer has any complete or consistent philosophy of life. It lives in fear of its pluralisms and resorts to expediency instead of principle to "keep the peace." It vacillates and compromises in its commitments and has become an enigma among the nations. Evidences of internal decay are being revealed which are startlingly similar to those which preceded the downfall of every major government in human history.

A Babel of clashing philosophies and ideologies are vieing for the control of men's minds.

Agnosticism is the prevailing philosophy of the masses. Ask the average man what he thinks about anything in the spectrum from God to Communism and he is most likely to say, "I don't know." People have suspended judgment because they feel they do not have sufficient knowledge to affirm or deny. The agnostic, of course, does not accept any authority. As an intelligent animal he seeks to profit by the wisdom of others and amasses mountains of knowledge to help him make up his mind. But the stance he assumes keeps him from accepting most of that wisdom and causes him to have doubts concerning its source. He can never be quite certain what is true, what is good or what is evil. He has no sense of sin, because he has no standard by which to evaluate and form a judgment. He admits that some kinds of conduct are desirable and some undesirable for pragmatic reasons, but circumstances and feelings are constantly changing his ideas of what is advantageous. He is unable to conceive of any act as worthy of punishment except it be for reformatory purposes. He has no fear of eternal punishment because he recognizes no divine law or no God to enforce it. The meaning of life, if he takes time to consider such a matter, is shrouded in his doubts. The average agnostic thinks that being alive is a chance circumstance of nature, that life in general has no particular purpose. As a person he has certain selfish objectives for which he is willing to fight in the spirit of Henley's, "I Am the Captain of My Soul," but he has no more hope of eternity than an ox. To most agnostics the ages-old philosophy of "eat, drink, and be merry, for tomorrow we die" is good enough to satisfy the healthy animal.

The agnostic mind is never completely satisfied. Despite its boasts and its foolhardy adventures it desires security. It is constantly exploring new philosophies. Agnostics might even consider the claims of Christianity if it were presented intelligently by people who acted as though they believed it. They are confused by the prejudice, hatred, greed, pride and pharisaism of many who call themselves Christian. If they could have confidence in the advocates and the examples of the Christian faith they might be willing to listen to its claims. But because of the educational and social background of the average agnostic he naturally turns to materialistic and humanistic philosophies.

Materialism is winning converts by the millions. It holds that all facts are causally dependent upon physical processes. Even facts about men's minds and wills and the course of human events are considered rather complicated phyiscal facts. Mental processes are determined by physical processes. The idea that a man can "make up his own mind" is foolishness to the materialist. Man reacts the way he does from bodily causes and there is really not much he can do about it. Materialists hold that men's thoughts and wishes may influence their own individual lives but that the course of human history is determined by the interaction of masses of men and masses of material things in such a way as to be predictable. The thing to do is to get in the main stream of events whether you like it or not.

Materialism is the basic philosophy of the Communist wave that is capturing the masses and infiltrating every nation under the sun. Communism insists that its way of life is the inevitable state of the future. We shall have more to say of Communism later.

The materialistic philosophy of Hegel largely influenced Karl Marx who is the foremost philosopher of modern Communism. Marx gave it the pragmatic twist that made it a dynamic force. But materialism is older than either Hegel or Marx. It figured in the fall of man recorded in the first chapters of Genesis. It is the temper of the mind that bows to the things which man apprehends by his "five senses." The Bible calls it "mammon." The materialist rates "him that taketh a city" higher than "he that ruleth his spirit."

Materialism can create all sorts of gods to which men will render allegiance. The State makes a good god for the Communist. Science makes a good god for other materialists. Other deities may be Wealth, Business, Power or Intellect. In these modern days materialism has provided all sorts of gadgets to make its gods attractive to the masses — men without conscience, without feelings, without scruples but with a bulldog determination to achieve success. The minds of the worshipers are nests of rationalizations in defense of their own gods, but of complete intolerance of the claims of others.

Materialism is the base for whole families of philosophies, all of which avoid God and the purposeful action of a Creator or Father in a being endowed with His attributes. These mechanistic ideologies assume that if atoms can be arranged in the proper chemical elements and space relations to each other in the fertilized ovum and if this embryo could then be placed in a proper physical environment, it would develop into a man. In other words, all these philosophies deal with man as a human animal and rely on matter and mechanical forces to explain all phenomena. They treat with scorn all those who accept the Bible as the Word of God. They bypass consideration of the nature of God, of life, of matter, of energy, of death or of anything else because they believe the acquirement of knowledge is merely a process of comparing phenomena.

Among these philosophies which appear to go beyond materialism is *humanism*. Humanistic views are quite attractive because they accord to man certain qualities of what they label the "human spirit." They suggest that there is such a thing as the perfectibility of human nature without recourse to supernatural aid. They propose moral and social programs to satisfy all worthy human needs and aspirations by removing all the harsh conditions of life. They stand for a certain emotional devotion to social reform and have produced many dedicated crusaders for the abolition of slavery, the liberation of women, the elimination of poverty, the creation of better conditions for labor, the better care and education of children, prison reform and the prevention of cruelty to animals. These modern-day humanists are philosophical kin to the humanists of the fourteenth and fifteen centuries who broke with the medieval tradition of philosophy and theology and made such a large contribution to literature, art, music, painting, sculpture, architecture and other forms of culture. Unfortunately, their material accomplishments were marred by worldliness, untamed passions and a lack of constructive social sympathy. All humanistic philosophies which seek to "lift man by his own boot straps" are limited to the importance of man's ego and to his faculties, affairs, temporal aspirations and well-being, and have no concern with eternity.

Idealism is the mother of another brood of philosophies. They are of such wide variety that it is difficult to fit them into any single pattern. While all of them seek to establish a view of the world which will lay foundations for a rational "religion," they are not necessarily committed to belief in a personal God or, indeed, to be-

lief in any particular god. Hegel, the great materialistic philosopher, called himself an idealist. Marx also thought of his views
as idealistic. The word "ideal," in its original Greek meaning, had
to do with the visible or material form, and was not primarily concerned with the eternal, infinite or immaterial. Yet because idealistic philosophies soar in speculative thought to "the wild blue
yonder" in search of a satisfactory religious solution to the co-
nundrum of life, they are not popularly considered materialistic.
Diderot once wrote: "We call idealists those philosophers who,
knowing only their own existence and that of the sensations that
follow one another in them, do not grant anything else . . . a system which, to the shame of the human mind and of philosophy, is
the most difficult to oppose although the most absurd of all. . . .
Whether we raise ourselves to the skies, whether we go down to
the bottom of the abyss, we never get outside ourselves." Whether
these idealistic philosophies are of the immaterial, phenomenal,
transcendental or absolute schools, they only lead to confusion and
agnosticism.

Idealism is the seedbed of much of the philosophical fadism that
infests the modern mind. The most popular of these current
thought fads is *existentialism.* It may well pass before this volume
is in covers, but it is nevertheless something to reckon with. The
plays of Tennessee Williams, Arthur Miller, Jean Paul Sartre; the
poetry of W. H. Auden, T. S. Eliot and Dylan Thomas; the painting of Picasso, Bracque, Mondrian, Miro and Kandinsky; the music
of Bartok, Milhaud, Hindemith; the architecture of Saarinen, Ru-
dolph and Le Corbusier — these are existentialist-inspired forces that
have shaped and are shaping the structure of the world in which
we live. A broad definition of existentialism is that it is a realistic
reaction against the shallow optimism of the old idealistic philosophies. Its spiritual father is Soren Kierkegaard who sat at the feet
of Hegel and accepted his idea of the alienation of man.* The

---

*Hegel taught that man's mind produces works of nature — art, science,
culture — and that man becomes alienated from society and himself in
these creations. To overcome this estrangement man must come to understand the nature of these productions so that the mind can come to
understand itself.

Danish philosopher held, however, that this alienation is not primarily mental or physical but spiritual, that if man attempts to overcome his estrangement he becomes an outcast from society and is condemned to a lonely walk with God while others walk the road of conformity. Existentialism in its modern disclosure is the fruit of an age of insecurity, devastated by two world wars and threatened by destruction in a third; an age of confusion and chaos without the certainties of the Christian faith. Its foremost modern advocates — Jaspers, Marcel, Heidegger, Sartre and De Beauvoir — are, without agreement among themselves, blind leaders of the blind. Jaspers and Marcel are nominal Christians and, like Kierkegaard, include God in their speculations. The others are atheists or agnostics who would encourage alienated man by drawing together all the consequences of a coherent agnosticism full of optimism and action. Despite their denials, existential philosophers are kept busy trying to prove that their system of thought does not plunge its disciples into further iconoclasm and despair. When existentialism ceases to be popular it will give place to some other faddist philosophy as futile as the rest. Each passing ideology leaves in its wake a disillusioned multitude and a society unable to find its way in a darkening world.

The most dangerous of all the theoretical philosophies of the day is *Communism*. It is most dangerous because it has become a dogmatic system involved in a religious crusade to lead humanity to a materialistic Utopia. As has already been stated, Communism is grounded in the materialistic idealism of Hegel. Karl Marx took Hegel's idea of alienation and constructed his own system of suppositions upon it. Marx held that man is alienated from his labor and that the only way he can assert his freedom is for all workers to unite in revolution to overthrow the *status quo* and assume ideological and political control of the world. Marx' system is called dialectical materialism. It excludes belief in the existence of God, of the soul of man, of the supernatural and of immortality. It holds the doctrine of economic determinism. It accepts Hegel's view of ideas and holds that the revolutionary philosophy is the thesis, the reactionary *status quo* is the antithesis and world revolution the synthesis — the victory of Communism and ultimate universal peace and prosperity. Lenin has interpreted Marxism in terms of the Russian revolution and the modern Communist Internationale.

Like other forms of materialistic idealism, Communism has created its own gods and developed its own religion. In the case of Communism this religion is a crude myth dogmatically imposed for the purpose of heightening the moral fervor of revolutionary action. In its essence it is unsupported by the disinterested survey of historical facts but since it unites a materialistic view of human nature with a moral passion for social reform, it has a tremendous dynamic in a confused and chaotic society. It has a special appeal to modern intellectuals for whom the old moral-religious traditions have become discredited and who believe that man and the whole universe can be explained in terms of natural science. The Communist religion has its basic law in the writings of Marx, Engels and Lenin. These "scriptures" have been canonized as holy writ which determines a distinct moral code, a new way of life, the goals of society and provides an orthodox technique by which these goals are to be achieved. The "church council" is the Congress of the Communist Party which determines the normative doctrine, which, in turn, is implemented by the Presidium and the Politburo. Deviations have all the qualities of old-fashioned "sin" and are punishable by banishment or death. Communism has produced a tremendous religious response among its millions of votaries. They are willing to sacrifice their lives, if need be, in a fanatical evangelistic crusade to make new converts and to undermine and destroy every institution or agency that stands in the way of ultimate victory for the cause. Dedicated Communists believe that they are in the main stream of predictable history and that the triumph of Communism is inevitable.

Communism's vision of its "heaven on earth" is far more intriguing to our materialistically minded generation than traditional religion's promise of so-called "pie in the sky." As soon as the revolutionary phase of movement has passed, Communist leaders are pledged to establish a Utopian socialistic society. They say it may take four, or five hundred years of propaganda, education, infiltration and deceit; or, if necessary, exploitation, robbery, pillage and brutality to overthrow class government and capitalist corruption. Then it will be necessary to establish a dictatorship of the proletariat until the masses are re-educated and all anti-Communist infection is liquidated. When this is done a homogeneous society will thrive in a prosperity based on the dictum "each according to his need, from each according to his ability." All production and all income will go to the State and be redistributed for the benefit of the masses, for the advancement of Communist ideals and for the enforcement of an orderly peace. Eventually, it is promised, the necessity for government will cease and society will be marked by universal peace and prosperity.

Propaganda and education with a purpose are at the heart of the Communist system. The press, the radio, television, movies, magazines, newspapers, novels, textbooks and every other medium of communication is used to soften up enemy nations — to confuse thinking, to weaken convictions, to downgrade nationalism and patriotism and to destroy religion. Every movement, organization, institution or segment of society is subject to infiltration and the dissemination of Communist doctrine. Communist agents establish cells, fronts and other instrumentalities where Communist doctrines are taught, members are recruited and from which Communist action is directed. In Communist lands education is given high priority. The method is indoctrination in basic principles and academic freedom in the development of the natural sciences provided the purposes of the State are served. As ancient Israel taught the Law, Communist states demand that from childhood their subjects be taught as they awake in the morning, taught as they go to bed, taught in the way, taught every day. (Russia has its "Sunday schools" in Communist doctrine.) To achieve its goals, Communist education employs systematically and deliberately all the tested principles of psychology, psychiatry and pedagogy. Only those who pass rigid tests are allowed to proceed to higher grades and finally to the universities. The intellectually incompetent are eliminated and assigned to various appropriate forms of employment. All sorts of incentives to educational attainment are offered and the State provides all the necessities of life free of charge. It is an educational system which builds discipline on set moral principles which the student must accept without equivocation and as meaningful to the good life. This set of values must guide him in his private and public behavior at all times and under all circumstances in the knowledge that deviation will be punished. The pupil is inspired, by the examples of Communist heroes, to courage, faith and a sense of personal responsibility. He is taught to think of himself as a pioneer in the redemption of society and an instrument in the achievement of Utopia.

Since the Red Russian revolution in 1917 Communism has spread with such rapidity that it now dominates more than one-third of the population of the globe. There is not a nation under the sun where its influence is not at work. Every year sees new territory annexed to its burgeoning empire. Its international leaders freely prophesy that the Red juggernaut will eventually "bury" America and that the children of this generation will live in a Communist society.

Naive, artless Americans and untutored, trustful Christians are often beguiled into believing that what has happened elsewhere cannot happen here. But it is happening in a society which is so weakened by the blandishments of conflicting ideologies and the impotence of the Christian churches that it is increasingly incapable of resisting the corroding materialistic, socialistic and communistic influences at work in every area of American life. The disconcerting thing about our situation is the growing number of distinguished scholars who counsel objectivity and neutrality. They are crusaders for rational enlightenment. They urge the claims of science, technology, power, freedom of the human spirit and wealth. They glorify scientific gains, inventive advance in mechanical gadgetry and instruments of power. They express the pious hope that the forces of sanity may prevent their use for the destruction of mankind. But when it comes to wholehearted commitment to any moral or religious position their attitude is nil.

They affirm their hospitality to all ideas and encourage objective discussion but are not prepared to accept conclusions as valid guidance. Everything, including God, is open to question. In the spirit of Bertrand Russell they intimate that no one should feel absolutely certain about anything.

With such "leadership" the wandering American will continue to be "tossed to and fro, and carried about with every wind of doctrine, by the sleight of men, and cunning craftiness." He will be the easy prey of the Communist menace unless he is confronted by the sure word of the true Christian faith.

It may be that this is the hour for the Christian Church to arise in the spirit which characterized the Christian movement in the first three centuries of its existence and initiate a moral and spiritual educational crusade of large proportions. Sir Richard Livingstone, for many years Vice-Chancellor of Oxford University said to an American religious leader recently, "When you and I were young there were moral fences that marked the road of life. We did not always keep to them. But we always knew when we crossed them. Today all the moral fences are down, and look at the world. Your job and mine is to build anew those fences so that we can keep to the road that will lead us out of the wilderness."

Chapter IV

THE NEW FREUDIAN ETHIC

IN the midst of ideological confusion and futility America finds itself in a moral vacuum. As Dr. Robert E. Fitch recently put it, in *Christianity and Crisis,* we live in "an age when ethics is becoming obsolete. It is superseded by science, deleted by psychology, dismissed as emotive by philosophy; it is drowned in compassion, evaporates into aesthetics and retreats before relativism. . . . The usual moral distinctions are simply drowned in a maudlin emotion in which we have more feeling for the murderer than for the murdered, for the adulterer than for the betrayed; and in which we begin to believe that the really guilty party, the one who somehow caused it all, is the victim, not the perpetrator of the crime."

Modern secular education and much of so-called religious education, which formerly gave the nation some semblance of moral leadership, is so obsessed by "the scientific spirit" that it maintains a deadly objective and neutral attitude toward ethics. It has much to say about our "pluralistic society." It informs about the different standards of morality and the varied social customs of the many ethnic, national and religious elements in the "new America." It sniffs at Puritanism and "the antiquated Protestant ethic." It cannot and will not say that there is such a thing as a sovereign God or a divinely revealed moral code. It fails to give any straightforward certain answer to the questions, Is this good? Is this evil? Is this right? Is this wrong? This agnostic attitude in the face of the burning fundamental issues of modern life is positively malevolent and contributes to the delinquency of society.

Yet this kind of education is unwittingly, or not, providing an ethic by which the masses are living. It is not easy to state it precisely because it is not precisely taught. It is an ethic that has eventuated in the absence of ethical and religious guidance. It is grounded in a mood that grips men when they begin to think of themselves as animals, with an animal ancestry and an animal destiny. The new ethic begins with the idea that nature is the ultimate reality, then moves on to the conviction that man is essentially an animal, that truth and right are relative and constantly changing. The pleasure of the moment, the pleasure of a lifetime, the pleasure of the group, the preference of the strongest are among the determinants of conduct.

Sigmund Freud is the high priest of this new amoral cult. This eminent Viennese psychologist, building on a godless philosophy and a naturalistic evolutionary biology, held that man descended from an ape ancestry and comes into this world unfit to meet the conditions laid on him by modern society. Man, said Freud, is not a responsible being. The best he can do is to adjust himself to the life imposed upon him by birth and environment. He has no soul. He is not to blame for his behavior. There is no objective or moral or spiritual norm to guide or restrain him. Life, according to the idol of many modern intellectuals, is just one neurosis after another. There may be salutary adjustments to ease man's condition but death is really man's only hope. This doctrine in some form or other can be detected in all the popular philosophies of life.

Freudian influence in psychology has given rise to the purely mechanistic views of many specialists in that field. Mind is held to be a material epi-phenomenon of the human body functioning with fixed stimuli. It has no innate self-consciousness or sense of God and is incapable of recognizing truth or error, right or wrong. Human conduct is said to be the result of fixed physical laws operating mechanically. Moral codes and the concept of sin are meaningless in such a system and in some instances are viewed as obstacles to man's well-being. The greatest good for the individual and society is believed to be achieved through the development of desirable nervous reflexes.

Even so-called Christian psychologists, who have shrunk from accepting naked Freudianism, adopt a syncretism of Christian and behavioristic views in which religious phenomena and human conduct are best explained by the action and reaction of the five senses, rejecting the spiritual realities without which moral compulsions became merely social convenience. They speak of the influence of ideals in conduct control but they often make ideals synonymous with habits. They insist that desirable reflexes of the nervous system are similar to idealistic thought conceptions. The logic of their naturalism weakens belief in a personal God and man's self-conscious ability to discern good from evil and therefore to make moral choices.

Sociology has been greatly influenced by Freudian doctrine, particularly in the field of social psychology. Much of modern sociology ignores the Christian teaching concerning man and his relationships with God and other men. It considers lightly the facts of history, anthropology, geography, economics, political science and cold statistics. Man is dealt with apart from his traditional behavior, faith, mores and philosophies. Too often he is considered as a faceless, malleable animal — the creature of social submissiveness to the changing social order. The approaches of this school of modern sociology to the solution of social problems are crassly biological, behavioristic, collectivistic and psychiatric. As the materialistic desires of societies and nations grow more intense and law and morality grow weaker, this type of sociology has only speculations to offer. The materialism of the age is rationalized into the acceptable fiction of the "economic" or "organization" man. The dignity of man is seen to consist in his status, or standard of living, rather than in his moral and spiritual endowments or standards. It is quite common these days to hear sociologists insisting that juvenile delinquency is not the fault of the individual but of society or that alcoholism, gangsterism, sex perversion and the like are due to social deficiencies. Societal disciplines are said to be repressive and therefore evil. Crime is a disease of society and criminals should be treated as patients rather than responsible persons. Such sociological doctrines have become powerful instruments in the hands of educators, scientists and experts in social welfare to propagate a purely materialistic, deterministic and amoral concept of man for sinister selfish or political ends.

America's system of higher education, long committed to evolutionary theory as the basis of scientific thought, was easy prey to the Freudian ethic. Large numbers of capable scholars have expelled God and the Bible from their philosophy of education and rejected moral and spiritual standards in dealing with human problems. They regard man as a human animal which may be influenced by external stimuli or experiences. They reject fixed standards or value judgments for the guidance of human conduct. They affirm the absolute conviction that there are no absolutes, no God-given rights, no ultimate truths. This basic philosophy of educational leaders has emerged in textbooks on psychology, sociology, education, history, economics, political science, literature and the fine arts. Students are deprived of instruction in any intelligible conception of an omnipotent and benign Supreme Being who has laid down certain immutable natural laws, endowed men with inalienable rights, and revealed unchallengeable basic rules of human conduct. They are thus denied any dependable criteria for evaluating right and wrong, good and evil.

It is small wonder that many surveys of pupils enrolled in modern public institutions of higher education reveal an amoral complex. One such survey of 27 schools and 3,500 students showed that 12 per cent did not consider stealing particularly wrong; 9 per cent would not agree that robbery is an act of juvenile delinquency; 15 per cent condoned vandalism; 17 per cent saw nothing wrong in sex abuses; 75 per cent thought lying and cheating essential to survival and success in modern society.

The promotion of this Freudian ethic among measurably mature young people in colleges and universities is debatable, but to foist it upon children and youths of limited intellectual capabilities who may be easy victims of questionable doctrines without parental consent is little short of perfidious. The vast numbers of boys and girls enrolled in elementary and secondary public schools are denied any sort of moral or spiritual instruction, yet they are exposed to doctrines which logically tend to destroy all desire for the development of their inner spiritual nature and leave them without the moral and spiritual undergirding so essential to meet the stresses of life which will inevitably beset them.

Dr. James Bryant Conant, whose interest in public education is widely valued, says: "Unless the educational progress includes at every level of maturity some continuing contact with those fields in which value judgments are of prime importance, it must fall far short of the ideal.—The student . . . must be concerned, in part at least, with the word 'right' and 'wrong' in both the ethical and mathematical sense." This ideal is being undermined and destroyed by the new ethic before it can scarcely be born in the lives of oncoming generations. The cold, hard facts concerning the social behavior of the generation trained in the Freudian educational atmosphere of American education speak for themselves: the highest divorce rate in the history of divorce statistics; the steady increase in crime among those under twenty-one; the sharp growth of juvenile delinquency; the amazing number of young men and women who are psycho-neurotics; the burgeoning necessity for larger and larger sanitoria and public asylums for mental derelicts; the strange allergies to individual initiative, hard work and sacrifice for high ideals; the growing agnosticism of the masses; the tragic nominalism apparent in church membership; the staggering complex of strange moral and social philosophies which repudiate the traditional Christian and American way of life.

In every area of society the fruits of the Freudian ethic have had startling effects.

In the *family* all the Judeo-Christian mores are under fire. Marriage is weakened by the growing belief that sexual deviations and pre-marital intercourse are justifiable. Common-law marriages are no longer thought sinful since physical union is believed to make a couple one. Intercourse, once sacred to the marriage chamber, is condoned wherever and whenever the compelling inner attitudes and motives of the participants appear to be mutually desirable. Divorce is considered a necessity in the search for compatibility. Discipline of children according to a moral or religious code of conduct is considered repressive and destructive of balanced mental and physical development. Parental authority is considered a relic of tribal culture.

In the area of *human welfare* many believe that rational thinking and social revolution are the only hope of mankind. With one foot in humanism and the other in science, modern programs of mental health bypass religion and deal with men as human animals. Security cannot be earned, say the experts, it must be achieved by government through the redistribution of wealth and the maintenance of mankind in reasonable comfort on economic levels which do not vary too widely. With a great show of concern, public monies are provided for the unfortunate only to be used for the creation of new social problems. For example, unwed mothers often use relief checks to entice professional gigolos into becoming fathers of more children so that comfortable living may be provided at public expense.

In *government* the sovereignty of God is being denied. The moral or natural law given by the Sovereign of the universe to all mankind has hitherto been considered basic to the fundamental and statutory law of the nation. It has been generally agreed that primary law is founded by infinite wisdom and goodness on essential righteousness which never varies and requires no amendment or alteration. Courts now tend to repudiate this concept and see the province of jurisprudence as wholly contained within the framework of man-devised law suited to the social mores of the times. Self-evident truth is bypassed for the rule that all concepts are relative and subject to change. Everywhere laws are being written to eliminate the old and incorporate the new. The very foundations of constitutional government are being shaken.

In *business* there are unmistakable signs of moral sag. A prominent executive in a recent luncheon conversation said, "I find that things have come to such a pass that when you remind businessmen that what they do is unethical by the old standards they simply shrug their shoulders and reply, 'Well, by the old rules perhaps, but it's legally permissible, so what?'" Thousands of chislers operate on a scale ranging from paltry deceptions of padding their tax returns to grandiose schemes on an international scale for tax avoidance. Bribes, price fixing, secret commissions, cutbacks, splits and dubious payoffs are common. A businessman who refuses to go along with such practices is called a "panty-waist" and a "relic" of the "horse and buggy" days.

In *labor* unscrupulous leaders feather their nests with a lion's share of the dues of the toiling masses. Gangsters who use murder and boycott as their weapons control crucial labor organizations, thus endangering the national defense and human welfare. The voices raised for Christian social justice are smothered in the self-seeking, capitalist-hating, power-mad propaganda that builds bigger unions at the expense of the public.

In *international relations* historic ideals of justice are being abandoned for methods of expediency. The bargaining method, the method of compromise, is superseding the mighty power of moral principle. In the first decade of the twentieth century many of the major nations of the world had signed a pact to outlaw war, only to see the world's bloodiest war fought to an inconclusive advantage. Now a ruthless cold war threatens to sap the vitals of Western civilization. Genocide continues to be practiced on a wide scale, whereby whole cultures are being wiped out. To use Professor Sorokin's phrase, mankind's questioning of all dogma has led to the demoralization of all peoples of all religions and those who have no religion. The ensuing easy materialism is no match for the fanatical zeal with which atheistic and materialistic Communism promotes its ends, even to the use of brutality and extermination.

In *culture and the fine arts* God and morality are generally missing. Illegitimacy has captured the legitimate theater. Of the thirty-five thousand motion pictures unveiled in the last twenty years hardly a score had religious plots and most of the rest were subversive of public or private morals. Painting, once patronized by the Church, has catered to the prurient interest or degenerated into impressionism. Great religious music has received no major contribution for decades while jazz, rock-and-roll and the rhythm beats of the Hottentots have captured the popular interest.

It would take a whole chapter to adequately delineate the effect of the Freudian ethic upon *religion* in general. Prayer has become a reflex influence or an escape mechanism. The Bible is widely believed to be of human origin to such an extent that it is no longer accepted as the revelation of God's will for man and the ultimate written authority for faith and life. God is viewed as being little more than the personification of the best in human relationships. Since conditioned reflexes determine all our acts, there can be no such thing as sin. Christ is still acknowledged to be a great moral leader but the idea of His being God manifest in the flesh or Redeemer from sin is considered an antiquated theological aberration. The evolving Church is busy adjusting itself to changing times and human needs. No wonder Ben Hecht, writing in *Esquire,* observed that "we need a new god for the space age" and that "the most amazing event to enter modern history has been generally snubbed by the chroniclers — it is the petering out of Christianity."

In this new Freudian climate millions of Americans exist with little or no concern for a higher and better life. They are victims of a loose and undefined atheism or agnosticism, neither believing nor disbelieving in the existence of a God. Only when they are confronted by some enormous crisis do they stop to think of the possibility of a spiritual dimension to life. They respect men of polished manners, brilliant minds and smooth address, who are skilled in the psychological art of persuasion. These blind leaders of the mind treat moral and spiritual matters in a delicate and inoffensive manner, putting thoughtful inquiries aside with a gentle sneer and stifling the stirrings of conscience with a sophisticated smile.

But the eclipse of the Christian ethic in our day is by no means total. There are other millions of Americans who are seriously concerned about the world crisis and their unpreparedness to meet its potential threats to the good life. Others advancing in years find it difficult to adjust themselves to changing situations and to find a rationale for life. Youth bored by routine, never quite sure of what they want to do, frittering away their lives in the quest of satisfying sensations, are "coming to themselves" like an earlier "prodigal son." These people are turning to the Church for help. The Christian churches have within them an immense potential of fully committed people who can be inspired, taught and led into a finer demonstration of the superiority of the Christian way of life and enlisted in a crusade to win others to Christ as Saviour and Lord.

The sentence with which Dante began *The Divine Comedy* is descriptive of our modern predicament: "In the middle of the journey of this life, I came to myself in a dark wood, where the direct way was lost." Is the Church failing to point out intelligently and convincingly the Way, the Truth and the Life?

Chapter V

SOUND OF MARCHING

TWICE in the Old Testament there appears the story of the victory of David over the Philistines in the valley of Rephaim. It marked a turning point in the death struggle of the Chosen People against seemingly superior forces. God instructed David, "Go not up after them; turn away from them, and come upon them over against the mulberry trees. And it shall be when thou shalt hear a sound of marching in the tops of the mulberry trees, then thou shalt go out to battle: for God is gone forth before thee to smite the host of the Philistines."

Today, for the Christian Church, there is a sound of marching. There are many encouraging signs of God's undertaking for His people, many encouraging signs of new life in the Church itself. There is a growing awareness of the deep trouble which threatens Christianity, a deepening concern about the future and an earnest seeking for a way out. Truly great leaders are emerging — men who have experienced a new sense of personal obligation to Christ and the Church and who are willing to make whatever ventures of faith God may require for the revitalization of the Church.

Possibly the most daring of these ventures is the *Ecumenical Movement.* There have long been dreams of and yearnings for a completely united Church of Christ and many attempts to achieve it. William Temple, late Archbishop of Canterbury, great apostle of unity, used to say, "I believe in one, holy, catholic Church and regret very much that it does not at present exist . . . but there was one Church and eventually again there will be one Church." He was thinking in terms of organic unity, a visible unity which would demonstrate the inner spiritual unity of the body of Christ which all admit. This outward unity which all the world can see is the kind of unity which the modern Ecumenical Movement seeks. The breakdown of the old institutional brands of Christianity now so apparent has already resulted in major changes in the life and structure of the Church. Dr. W. A. Visser 't Hooft says: "The real motivation of the ecumenical movement was a sense of repentance that in the actual life of the churches the holiness, the apostolicity, the unity of the Church has been obscured; and a determination to manifest more clearly the true nature of the Church of Christ." There is a wide feeling that the time is long past due when hair-splitting doctrinal differences, bigotry, intolerance and outmoded traditions must no longer be permitted to keep Christians from worshipping together and working together in the main functions and tasks of the Church. Such a movement should have the prayers and active interest of all who profess to be followers of Christ.

The chief problem in effecting organic unity appears to be institutional. The tendency in many ecumenical circles is to minimize creed and theology. There is search for "the least common denominator" or an "acceptable symbolism" in these areas. It is hoped that the ultimate structure will incorporate the best in the Catholic, Reformed and Evangelical traditions and be subject to the principle of continuing change, so that "God may reveal Himself and His will more and more completely" through the Church as the years pass. These ecumenists see the proposed Church as open to all who profess faith in Christ and recognize each other as belonging to the people of God. This might be comparatively easy to realize because of the widespread lack of Bible knowledge and Christian conviction. The institutional problems which defy easy solution are mutual recognition of ministerial ordinations; reconstruction of connectional bodies — presbyteries, sessions, synods, conferences, conventions, assemblies; merging of boards, corporations, foundations, endowments and institutions; the creation of a central authority for the direction of a responsible Church program, without the sacrifice of democracy and freedom.

The road to ecumenical achievement will be a long one. There is grave doubt whether the churches can wait on ecclesiastical restructuring in a time of crisis which calls for immediate action. Then, too, there is grave fear that concern for the organic unity of the Church may weaken regard for the Christian witness, the preaching of the Gospel, instruction in the Holy Scriptures, personal commitment to the living Christ and crusade for the salvation of the world. In some quarters there is a growing feeling that Christians should not spend the next ten or twenty years in ecumenical concerns and after that make a united thrust for Christ in a pagan world. The chief task of the Church — education and evangelism — must be its chief task now.

Revival is spreading in many areas of the Church's life. It is a well-known fact of Church history that Christianity has been at its liveliest best when stirred by a mighty heaven-sent revival. From the days of Peter and Paul, down through those of Savonarola to those of Billy Graham huge crowds have heard great preachers of righteousness call sinners to repentance and plead for the salvation of souls. Lives have been changed and the power of the Gospel demonstrated so graphically that whole communities and nations have been transformed.

The hallmark of evangelical revival has been the preaching of the Christ of the Cross, the sacrifice of the Lamb of God to take away the sin of the world. The multitudes become conscious of their guilt and realize there is no forgiveness except in the shed blood of Christ, that there is no reconciliation with God without the atonement and no eternal life apart from Christ crucified, buried, raised and alive forevermore. Out of the salvation experience of the great revivals comes urgency to share it with others. The fires of true revival sweep from life to life until there is spiritual conflagration and the Church becomes afire for God. The Church in the modern world should be praying earnestly for genuine revival. Never was there a more crucial need.

But there are "rifts within the lute" of much of modern evangelism. Much of it is theologically hollow. Preachers have sought more to set the emotions of their hearers afire than to teach God's plan of salvation and secure an intelligent acceptance of Christ as Lord and Saviour. John Wesley, who was one of the greatest evangelists of all time, once wrote: "Let but a pert, self-sufficient animal, that has neither sense nor grace, bawl out something about Christ and His blood or justification by faith, and his hearers cry out, 'What a fine gospel sermon.'" Even when there is a genuine "turning to the Lord," much of modern evangelism fails to provide essential Bible teaching for its converts that they "may be perfect, thoroughly furnished unto all good works." Christ inseparably linked teaching with evangelism. If teaching is neglected, faith will have no roots in intelligent understanding and will soon wither and die. Naive and uninformed Christians are no match for the sophisticated materialists who dominate modern society.

Too much of modern evangelism is staged by elaborate organization and promoted by methods reminiscent of the high-powered techniques of Madison Avenue. The plea, "Be not conformed to this world," is muffled by worldly standards of revival success and ambitious status-seeking. There is insistence on the "new birth" and the necessity of taking a pietistic stand amid the worldliness of a pagan society, but the resulting "conversions" are too often indistinguishable from the unconverted hoi polloi. High-powered "visitation evangelism" drives in local parishes produce remarkable numerical results, but the new members who lied, cheated, gossiped, drank and partied before they signed their "covenant cards" too often continue their delinquencies. The community cynics are unimpressed with the values of "commitment to Christ." Affiliation with church is looked upon as a mere formality rather than a life-changing event. The ecclesiastical vocabulary of the evangelist employs all the traditional and biblical words in his campaign or crusade but they are too often meaning-less symbols of an unrealized experience.

It is manifestly the duty of the Church to correct this situation and to use every means at its command to mount revival, but is it not possible that educational evangelism offers the most effective media for extending the Kingdom in this modern world?

Another bold venture which seeks to give new life and purpose to a lagging Christianity is the *Social Gospel movement*. It was born in a day of industrial and intellectual revolution when prog-ress was believed to be inevitable and man essentially good. It represented a shift from Christian concern for the redemption of the individual to the redemption of society. The Social Gospel en-visions a Utopia, not the fruitage of a Marxist philosophy, but the realization of the Kingdom of God on earth.

Changing times have given strong impetus to this new Gospel. Its preachers see themselves in the role of the ancient Hebrew prophets crying out against the evils of society and pointing the way toward a new day when "swords shall be beaten into plow-shares" and everyone will live in peace "under his own vine and fig tree." They see the Church adding its moral force to the social and economic forces already at work, and in a time of "malleable heat" shaping humanity into the good life. They would lift the Church out of its narrowness and provincialism into the full sweep and thrill of social revolution. They believe that the spirit of Christianity in the modern world should be that of a triumphant faith proclaiming the sovereignty of Christ in all human affairs and His enthronement in a new social order.

Dr. Walter Rauschenbusch, one of the most brilliant leaders of the movement, once said: "The religion of Jesus has less to fear from sitting down at meat with publicans and sinners than from the immaculate isolation of the Pharisees. . . . If the Church tries to confine itself to theology and the Bible, and refuses its larger mission to humanity, its theology will become a mythology and its Bible a closed book." Rauschenbusch and his disciples feel that if society continues to disintegrate and decay the Church will be carried on with it, but if the Church can rally the moral forces of society, injustice will be overcome and fresh blood will give new life to the nation. In the process the Church itself will rise to "higher liberty and life."

But the Social Gospel has come through some hard times. Its Utopian social constructs of the future have paled into insignificance alongside the glowing prospects of the welfare state. Church-sponsored political programs have failed to solve social problems. Many are beginning to realize that the Church cannot offer political salvation. While its representatives lobby and engage in political action, the public scorns such a role and calls on the Church to be the Church. Partisan agencies often reap the harvest of its labor and use social gains as steppingstones to political power. It becomes more and more apparent even to the Church that righteousness cannot be legislated. The "Kingdom of God on earth" seems as far away today as when the Social Gospel movement began.

As something of a reaction against the shifting stance of the Social Gospel and the uncertain faith of its advocates the Church is showing a new interest in *theology*. The positive message of the Holy Scriptures has become once more a major concern of modern Christians. Theology is, or should be, "the exhibition of the facts of Scripture in their proper order and relation, with the principles and the general truths involved in the facts themselves and which pervade and harmonize the whole." Theology has given vertebrate strength to the Christian faith that highlights the personality and creatorship of God; His purpose in love and grace; sin as the distortion of divine-human relations; Jesus Christ as the incarnation of the eternal Word; His sufferings and death as the atonement for sin; His present activity as the supreme power in the Christian's life; the right of Christ to eternal lordship; the obligation of the Christian to proclaim Christ everywhere as the Way, the Truth and the Life; and His coming again to judge the world. The great historical creeds of Christendom have phrased these fundamentals of the Christian faith in various ways, but in essence this is the ground of theology.

Christianity has lived under various cultures and many forms of government and society. It has continued to exist through the rise and fall of eras, cultures, institutions, constitutions, empires and civilizations. But its basic truths have remained essentially the same. It has an infinite capacity of maintaining their relevance to any situation within the scope of divine providence. Theology expresses Christian faith in terms which meet the needs of men in every period of history. It lays down principles of unity for all men in God. It offers a remedy for sin which is responsible for keeping the world in strife. It sets up a moral and spiritual standard of evaluation and judgment. It gives valid reasons for man's existence and clarifies his future destiny. It is little wonder, therefore, that in these crisis times there should be a renewed interest in theology. The future can always be as bright for the Christian as his knowledge of God and the purposes of God.

Historically the main stream of theology has been biblical. It has been drawn from the clear teachings of the Holy Scriptures. Its assumptions and conclusions have been measured by the divine standard. But through the centuries brilliant theologians have built up various schools of thought with a bewildering variety of doctrinal systems and sectarian institutions which obscure rather than clarify the comparatively simple theology of the Bible itself. While the return to theology is an encouraging evidence of hunger for the deeper things of God and a search for sure foundations of faith, it is filled with dangers of intensifying traditional differences and further confusing the minds of average Christians. On the other hand, non-biblical theologians, with their theological fadisms rising and fading with popular tastes, leave their disciples disillusioned and adrift in a mild agnosticim.

Theology in depth can never be a substitute for the simplicity of Scriptural statement of divine truth implemented in daily Christian living. The great masses of men will never respond to the hair-splitting points of theological disputation, but they will eagerly search the Scriptures for the outlines of the divinely revealed theology which they can apprehend and upon which they can build an abiding personal faith in the Lord Jesus Christ.

There is a sound of marching in the area of *Christian education*. There are approximately eight hundred liberal-arts colleges related in some way to the Protestant churches in the United States. Another two hundred colleges of distinctly evangelical persuasion have recently come into existence and are growing rapidly. In general it can be said that these institutions are manifesting a revitalization of the distinctly Chritian education which has made such a large contribution to the life of the Church and the nation.

Higher education in America had its beginnings in church-related schools. While Harvard was not distinctly sectarian, it was conceived, according to its charter of 1650, for the purpose of educating youth "in knowledge and godliness," an aim summed up in its twin mottoes of *Veritas* and *Christo et Ecclesia*. Yale, founded in 1701, declared its purpose to be the preparation of young men for service in "Church and civil State." Dartmouth, Columbia, Princeton and scores of other colleges might be cited as evidence of the fact that the founding fathers of the nation were convinced that Christian ideals and principles were basic to sound education. Wherever churches were established on the new frontiers, ministers founded schools many of which grew into major colleges.

The secularization of many of these schools and a majority of the other institutions of higher education now in existence followed the trends in American life which have been depicted in earlier chapters in this book. But this change in no way invalidates the principle that without true Christianity the cultural enterprise cannot maintain its highest standards or reach its true fulfillment.

The Christian Church is beginning to realize in a most encouraging way that if its money is to be given to support the higher-educational enterprise, it has a right to expect that it be distinctly Christian. If worthy of the name Christian, a college must deal with thought and life in a Christian context. It must not be objective or neutral with regard to pagan and secular theories of reality and history and must be devoted to the biblical view of God, of man and of the world.

God, instead of science, is the central and normative factor in education in these distinctly Christian institutions of higher education. Science has been the most powerful influence in the promotion of secularism. It has encouraged a lopsided view of human nature and experience. It has tended to eliminate faith in the supernatural and has considered the brain as a kind of machine for grinding out general facts and knowledge, learning more and more of less and less. When God is central, true science is encouraged and given deeper meaning. Courses in the Bible, Christian theology, Church history and other studies designed to establish moral and spiritual stability, complete a curriculum which serves the full-orbed life and gives essential unity in a meaningful cosmic totality.

The effect of moral instruction in these institutions is most encouraging. Released from cold scientific and materialistic concepts of life, value judgments are once more being made on the basis of biblical ethical standards. Convinced that the inner character is not automatically the result of greater knowledge, provision is made for chapel services and Christian-emphasis weeks in which the claims of Christ are laid upon the hearts of the student bodies. Opportunities are being provided for the demonstration of Christian ideals individually and socially, both on campus and in community projects.

Bible institutes and Bible colleges are a distinctive new development in Christian higher education in America. These institutions represent the reaction of right-wing Protestant churches and interchurch groups to the secularization and theological apostasy of the older church-related colleges. Their earliest interest was the training of a new Christian leadership, but with the passing years they have broadened their educational concern. Many of them now offer a well-balanced curriculum in the liberal arts and religion centralized in a strictly biblical world view. It includes studies in the humanities, social and natural sciences but puts emphasis on direct Bible study. It is concerned with the American Christian heritage as against modern secularism and the encroachments of atheistic socialism and Communism. Dr. Frank E. Gaebelein, in *Christian Education in a Democracy*, characterizes this unique movement as a reassertion of "the primacy of religion in educating for life. Bound neither by the graveclothes of classicism nor the chains of empirical science, Bible-college education makes use of the abiding elements of both while providing an integrated education for the whole man."

While the current trends in Christian higher education are encouraging and should be adequately supported by the Church, they are far from sufficient to cope with the rising tides of secularism. They only indirectly affect the grass roots of American life. The community leadership of graduates from Christian colleges and universities is usually exceeded in numbers and popular acceptance by graduates from secular institutions where humanistic and materialistic philosophies are favored. In many communities the well-educated Christian element is all but lost in a predominantly secular society. There is need for some mass movement in Christian education at the grass-roots level which can speedily effect a change in this pagan climate.

There are encouraging sounds of marching in the field of Christian education at the local church level. In recent years there has been a serious effort to improve its teaching and training efficiency. Academic disciplines have been introduced. Higher standards for teachers and leaders have been set up. Improved curriculum materials have offered more Bible content, utilized the best in modern pedagogical methods and provided means for a more systematic and effective spiritual nurture.

The evangelical sector of the Sunday-school movement has shown remarkable vitality. Great emphasis has been laid on indoctrination in the fundamentals of the Christian faith and their application to life in a changing world. Evangelism has been restored to its rightful position in the purpose and program of Christian education. Evangelical leaders equate education and evangelism and promote these twin functions of the Church simultaneously. This has resulted in a remarkable numerical growth in

Sunday-school enrollment and church membership. Pupils are being won to Christ in such numbers that they account for eighty per cent of the additions in evangelical churches each year. An aggressive community enlistment program has made a splendid impression on people who have had doubts concerning the vitality of the Church in these modern times. Spiritual emphasis characterizes the "new look" in evangelical Sunday schools. There has been a complete break with the naturalistic and coldly intellectual approach in religious education and a turn to the warmly personal and experiential appeal. A compelling spiritual warmth results in sacrificial and zealous commitment to Christ and the Church. Evangelicals see the Sunday school as a divine institution with divine oversight, a divine mission and a divine program. Churches and communities where this concept obtains are feeling the impact of a new dynamic.

But, unfortunately, in the average Sunday school there is only deadly conformity to traditional routine and a lamentable apathy concerning educational advance. There is no vision of enlargement adequate to the needs of the times. As encouraging as gains in this field may be, they leave much to be desired.

In the third volume of Winston Churchill's monumental work, *The Second World War*, he describes the night when he and his closest friends received word of the Japanese attack on Pearl Harbor. They had been enswathed in deepening gloom concerning the trends in the conflict which seemed to give little hope to the Allies. This new development further depressed everyone in the room except Churchill. The others saw only the lives lost, damage to prestige, the weakness of a potential ally. Churchill with his deep conviction that God was on his side, with his wide grasp of the cause-and-effect realities of history, felt that this was the turning point of the war, the weight in the balances which would bring America into the war. At Chequers that night was born a new conviction of victory.

There is unquestionably a "sound of marching in the mulberry trees" and the Lord will honor His people if they will follow His leadership. Fully convinced and dedicated Christians, who grasp the cause-and-effect realities of history and know that the times of religious and moral declension have always been followed by revival and advance, are certain that there is hope for eventual victory for Christ and the Church.

Even in these apocalyptical times — this is the victory that overcometh the world, *even our faith!*

Chapter VI

A LESSON FROM HISTORY

HISTORIANS and philosophers have written millions of pages on the revolutionary impact of Christianity upon society in the first three centuries of its existence.

Yet modern Church leaders, in their search for a solution of the modern world debacle, seem little concerned to discover why such a revolution took place. They seem to assume that this space age is so radically different that only science and the scientific method are adequate to the task of finding a way out.

They seem to ignore the fact that human nature is still basically the same as it was before A.D. 400 and that Christ is the same yesterday, today and forever. As Kierkegaard once put it, "It is always the imperishable which sustains the perishable, the spiritual which maintains the corporal." They seem unaware of the relevance of Toynbee's thesis that "the most important questions that men must answer are the questions on which science has nothing to say."

It has always been true that nations and civilizations have continued to exist only as long as they had an ethical purpose which served God and humanity. The great empires of Greece and Rome (and all those which preceded them) had moral cultures, codes and idealisms which sustained their objectives. When morality and religion decayed, the political and social structures disintegrated and finally collapsed.

Rome is one of the best examples of this postulate. Religion and morality were pagan but they possessed certain high idealisms which served the Empire well. Religion was destitute of high theological principles but borrowed heavily from the great philosophers of Greece and Rome whose ideas, strangely enough, find wide acceptance in certain sectors of our modern culture. Purity of mind and body were requirements of the good life. Devotees were expected to excel in decency and virtue, to be chaste in conversation, temperate in diet and maintain an honorable reputation. They were taught that the world is governed by the gods, that their goodness is the source of temporal blessing and that they have prepared a future state of reward and punishment for man's immortal soul.

When the day came that the fabulous temples of the Roman Empire were filled with lascivious rites and polluted with immoral practices, Rome was foredoomed to fall. The Apostle Paul in the first chapter of his letter to the Church in Rome depicts the degeneracy of society when Christianity was born. He said the people "became vain in their imaginations, their foolish heart was darkened, professing themselves to be wise they became fools . . . filled with unrighteousness, fornication, wickedness, covetousness, maliciousness, full of envy, murder, debate, malignity; whisperers, backbiters, haters of God, despiteful, proud, boasters, inventors of evil things, disobedient to parents, without understanding, covenant breakers, without natural affection, implacable, unmerciful. . . ."

Edward Gibbon in his monumental work, *The History of the Decline and Fall of the Roman Empire*, puts moral and religious decay among the chief reasons for the fall of Rome: the rapid increase of divorce, undermining the sanctity of the home, which is the basis of human society; the decay of religion, faith fading into mere form, losing touch with life and becoming impotent to guide it; the mad craze for pleasure, sports becoming increasingly exciting and brutal.

Gibbon also blamed higher and higher taxes, the spending of money for food and circuses, the building of gigantic armaments, the neglect of agriculture, political nepotism and other forms of corruption, but the great historian saw as the major problem the decadence of the people themselves.

Outwardly, at the time of Christ, Rome seemed prosperous and strong. It dominated practically all of the known world. Its imperial rule and system of jurisprudence were superb. Its splendor was marked by its innumerable public monuments, its magnificent temples and other architectural triumphs, its great highways linking key cities, its mammoth fleets, its mighty legions, and by the pomp and luxury enjoyed by its upper classes. But within the people themselves were the forces of evil which were inevitably to bring its downfall. Today ancient Rome is only dust and rubble.

Guglielmo Ferrari, in his *Ancient Rome and Modern America*, depicts a startling similarity of the elemental forces at work in both cultures and predicts the end of our civilization if some major moral and spiritual revolution does not change the course of modern events.

The Christian Church came to grips with Rome while Christ was still on earth. Rome sent Him to the Cross and cast His followers to the lions in an effort to stem the growth of doctrines and modes of conduct which were the very antithesis of Hellenic and Roman concepts. The Church had little or no wealth, social influence, political power or intellectual status. As an institution it was no match for the institutions of Rome, yet in three centuries Christianity triumphed over them and changed the whole course of human history.

What was the secret of this miraculous achievement? If we can discover the means by which Christianity won the conflict two thousand years ago with opposing forces which are basically identical with those challenging the Church today, we should be able to map a strategy adequate to our times.

Primarily, of course, the secret of triumph lies in the power of the Christian Gospel. It is not by human might, nor by power,

but by the Spirit of God that spiritual and moral victories are
won. However, God in His divine economy has chosen to use
men to accomplish His purposes. It will not be possible in this
limited study to discuss all the ways in which God works. Only
one, but withal a most important one, will engage our attention
— *Christian education.*

How did Christian education operate in the midst of the antagonistic society of the first three centuries of the Christian era?

Christ Himself set the basic pattern. Early in Christ's earthly
ministry, He was called "Rabbi." Ever since, He has been widely
acclaimed as the "Master Teacher." In the Synoptic Gospels alone,
He is addressed twenty-six times as Teacher. Before Peter's confession of His deity, He is depicted as "teaching," and twenty
times following that incident. The nature of His mission as
Messiah required that He instruct His followers concerning the
ground and validity of His claims. Moving on from this phase
of His teaching, He disclosed His own deeper self, His mission
and message, and the meaning and cost of discipleship. In His
appearances before the masses He preached the Gospel of the
coming Kingdom and accompanied His appeals with teaching
concerning that Kingdom.

The educational aim of Christ was to fit men to live in perfect
harmony with the revealed will of God. He was constantly
teaching men how to establish right relations with God and
how to live in full possession of divine power. He anticipated
every great leader of thought and every great teacher by declaring
that perfection is the true end of education. The Sermon on the
Mount is the epitome of that perfect life.

His teaching regarding the Kingdom set a goal which made
the pathway of learning alluring and romantic. In His first
public discourse at Nazareth He proclaimed good tidings for
the poor, release for the captives, recovery of sight to the blind,
liberty for the bruised and "the acceptable year of the Lord." The
doors of the Kingdom were open to all — rich and poor, educated
and ignorant, noble and plebian, Jew and Gentile, bond and free.
The citizens of the Kingdom would have equal rights, privileges

and rewards inasmuch as talent and ability are the only media through which men can give themselves to the service of God and humanity.

His program was Christ-centered. He was King in His Kingdom. He was the Way, the Truth and the Life. He was Water for the thirsty, Bread for the hungry, Light for those in darkness. Full allegiance and submission were essential and indispensable to His program. God's will, as revealed in Christ's teaching and in the Holy Scriptures of His time, was binding and obligatory upon every disciple. Learning this will was a major concern of the teaching process. Christ did not shrink from indoctrination. He spoke as one having authority and His fiat, "This do and thou shalt live," had no alternative. The other major educational concern was demonstration and action — doing the will of God. In obedience to His will was to be found the larger liberty which all men covet.

Christ's appeal to the human will was unique in education. None of the great teachers of history had gone so far in demands upon the pupil. The closing part of the Sermon on the Mount illustrates this fact:

"Not every one that saith unto me, Lord, Lord, shall enter into the kingdom of heaven; but he that doeth the will of my Father who is in heaven. Many will say unto me in that day, Lord, Lord, did we not prophesy by thy name, and by thy name cast out demons, and by thy name do many mighty works? And then will I profess unto them, I never knew you: depart from me, ye that work iniquity. Every one therefore that heareth these words of mine, and doeth them, shall be likened unto a wise man, who built his house upon the rock: and the rain descended, and the floods came, and the winds blew, and beat upon that house; and it fell not: for it was founded upon the rock. And every one that heareth these words of mine, and doeth them not, shall be likened unto a foolish man, who built his house upon the sand: and the rain descended, and the floods came, and the winds blew, and smote upon that house; and it fell: and great was the fall thereof. And it came to pass, when Jesus had finished these words, the multitudes were astonished at his teaching: for he taught them as one having authority, and not as their scribes."

Christ asked the world to judge Him and His teaching by what His followers did, by the fruits of His teaching in their life and conduct.

Christ made it clear that there were two ways, and two ways only, that men could live. One way was that of Christ, the Spirit and the Kingdom. The other was the way of the world, the flesh and the devil. One was the way of eternal life. The other was the way of death. This clear-cut division called for ethical choice and action, left no gray corridor for doubt and vacillation. It gave a graphic, consistent guide for daily living.

Christ's example in teaching and life became the pattern for education in the early Christian Church. There were no schools in the formal sense. The home and the church were the major educational media, but education was not confined to them. Christian education was a life experience. It took place in the midst of daily living and, especially because of the evangelistic nature of the Christian faith, moved out into the market place and the synagogue to make disciples of Christ from all walks of life. Indeed, the Great Commission called for educational adventure that carried the new faith and the new life "to the uttermost part of the earth."

Since Christianity had its beginnings in the center of the Jewish faith and its first converts came from a Jewish background, it is likely that Christian education followed some of the Hebrew practices. Every household was responsible for teaching. At an early age the child was initiated into a knowledge and observance of the instruction contained in the Sacred Writings. Paul, in writing to Timothy, recalls that he was taught by his grandmother, Lois, and his mother, Eunice. There were many evidences in early Christian literature that every Christian father and mother were required to bring up their children "in the nurture and admonition of the Lord." As the Hebrew child was taught the necessity of the blood sacrifice in the slaying of the paschal lamb during the Passover, the Christian child was instructed in the significance of Christ's death on the Cross for the redemption of mankind. The observance of the Lord's Supper was a means of instruction in this great central doctrine of the Christian Church. Children waited eagerly for the day when they would personally partake of the sacred emblems and enter into mystical relationship with the body of Christ. A child, fulfilling his obligation to his parents, committed to memory important passages of Christian truth which guided him in his daily conduct. Parental discipline was based on the Christian way of life. When the child was deemed old enough to read and study for himself, he was encouraged to develop his own thought and devotional life, under the guidance of the Holy Spirit, to make his own decision to accept Christ as Saviour and Lord and to become a full-fledged member of the Church.

The early Christian churches were composed of those who obeyed the terms of the Christian Gospel and their assemblies became centers of education, worship, fellowship, nurture and evangelism. Education was a major concern of the churches. In the Apostolic era of Church history the program of education was Christ-centered. The subject matter of teaching was the Word of God, which embraced the Old Testament Scriptures and the "apostles' doctrine" which they had received from Christ and His chosen disciples. Elders or presbyters were charged with educational responsibilities and well-qualified members were set apart as teachers. In the weekly meetings of the Church, instruction occupied a large place. Baptism and the Eucharist had their educational significance, reminding worshippers of the basic facts of the Gospel — the death, burial and resurrection of Christ. Church leaders insisted upon orthodox belief and a clean-cut break with the world in moral conduct. When there was digression, the dissident members were "instructed in the way of the Lord more perfectly" and, should conditions warrant, disciplinary action was taken. These early congregations were literally schools of Christ in which Christians "grew in grace and in the knowledge of the truth."

Preaching and teaching were closely associated in the work of the apostles and their immediate successors. The message itself was the *kerygma,* or the Gospel. It was both proclaimed and taught. The sermons consisted essentially of three parts. First was the statement of the salient facts of the Gospel. Paul states these in his first epistle to the church at Corinth: "I delivered unto you first of all that which I also received, how that Christ died for our sins according to the scriptures; that he was buried, and that he rose again the third day according to the scriptures, and that he was seen of Cephas, then of the twelve. . . ." The second part of the sermon consisted of the proofs of the Hebrew Scriptures and the testimony of witnesses to the passion and resurrection of Christ. The third division of the teaching called for belief in Christ, entrusting the whole life to Him, and obeying Him in all that He commanded. The elaboration of the *kerygma* involved the apostles' doctrine, or *didache.* There was constant need for interpretation of the Hebrew Scriptures in terms of the *kerygma.* Garbled interpretations of the Gospel began circulating among the churches, and its preachers and teachers had to be eternally vigilant in correctly expounding the Way. Gradually, through the medium of letters or epistles written by inspired teachers, the *kerygma* and the *didache* were committed to permanent forms which eventually came to compose the New Testament of the Holy Bible. This canon of authentic books then became the authoritative basis for all future instruction in the Christian Church.

In the early Church there were also "forms of teaching" or "doctrine," to which allusion has already been made. Foremost of these were Baptism and the Eucharist. Baptism was a constant reminder, a great object lesson in the death, burial and resurrection of Christ and also in the Christian's death to the world, the flesh and the devil; the burial of the "old man" and his resurrection as a "new creature" to "walk in newness of life." Christians saw in the observance of the Eucharist, or Lord's Supper, the bread reminiscent of the body of Christ broken for them and the wine typifying the blood of Christ shed for many for the remission of sin. The old idea of worship with its many elements of fear and restitution and its strict ritual was replaced with times of inspiration, instruction, spiritual renewal¹ and Christian fellowship. Other "forms of teaching" were briefly stated confessions of faith. Peter's confession, "Thou art the Christ" and its later elaboration, "I believe that Jesus is the Christ, the Son of the living God, and my personal Saviour" was probably the earliest. It has been suggested that the definition of the Gospel as briefly stated in I Corinthians 15:3-5, or similar words, was a form of confession which preceded Baptism and the observance of the Eucharist. The words of institution confessed the Holy Trinity. Later came the creedal hymn with its mention of "good teaching" and then the Apostles' Creed which outlines fundamental Christian doctrine. All these forms were of immense value in keeping clear the basic elements of the Christian faith.

The teaching of "the two ways" which Christ had so effectively used in His ministry was prominent in the educational technique of the primitive Church. The *Didache,* a manual believed to have been available to the churches in the first century, emphasized the instruction in the "way of life" and the "way of death." This was distinctly ethical in content and formed a pattern for Christian living as opposed to the pagan practices which so widely obtained at that time. The way of life included the virtues of kindness, meekness, love, faith, tenderness, lowliness of mind or humility, longsuffering, peace, patience, forgiveness, righteousness, self-control, likemindedness, joy, goodness, truth, compassion and brotherly love. The way of death included a list of sins: fornication, covetousness, malice, blasphemy, uncleanness or lewdness, strife, jealousy, anger, contentiousness, cupidity, adultery, lasciviousness, envy, idolatry, murder, theft, deceit, lying, confusion, gossip, backbiting, sorcery, drunkenness, reveling, divisiveness, extortion, haughtiness or arrogance, malignity, vainglory and injustice. It was this ethical teaching, backed by the conversion and baptismal experience of "the new birth," which shaped the lives of Christians and in turn literally changed the course of history. One of the earliest names for Christianity was "the way." Christ Himself in His perfect life was "the way." Christians were "followers of the way." They found their joy in living like Christ and in seeking to share that joy with others. It was not only in their daily relationship with the living Christ, but also in their relationship to their neighbors which began to mark Christians as "different" and to cause the community to ask the reason or the secret of their good life. Christians took a pardonable pride in being different, in non-conformity to the pagan mores, though never in a spirit of self-righteousness.

The Church's educational function became so important to its life that catechumenal schools eventually came into being. Persons receiving instruction were called catechumens. These schools provided a process of instruction for those who desired to become members of the Church but who lacked the requisite knowledge of Christian doctrine and ethics. In general the pupils were divided into two groups — those who merely expressed the desire for and those who were thought worthy of admission. Only after candidates had undergone instruction and discipline were they considered ready for baptism. These catechumens included children of believers, Jewish converts and adult converts from heathenism. The instruction for children was quite simple and was designed to supplement the teaching which was provided in the homes. Catechumenal instruction for Jews consisted chiefly in a Christian interpretation of the Hebrew Scriptures, in the Gospel of Christ, the Apostles' doctrine and in the two ways. The pattern for Gentiles probably began with the two ways because of the moral imperative and was followed by instruction in the Gospel and the Apostles' doctrine, then in the life of Christ and finally in the Greek versions of the Hebrew Scriptures pertaining to the Messiah. The root meaning of the word *catechumenoi* intimates a "sounding down" or a "singing out" which may have been descriptive of the early teaching practice of singing the answers to questions. This would indicate that indoctrination was highly favored as a means of inculcating divine truth. In another respect, some believe there was instruction in music and hymnody. The psalmody of the early Church, especially in the East, was of conspicuous importance. Christianity was a joyful, singing faith.

This type of school was the forerunner of the catechetical school which, in turn, was the precursor of the Sunday school.   Pure Christianity has always insisted on an educated constituency — one that knows basic doctrine, why Christian beliefs are superior to other beliefs, that knows its basic ethical code and is intent on winning others to Christ.

The effect of the Christian way of life upon the corrupt society of the early centuries following the birth of Christ was tremendous. Dr. Paul Monroe, eminent historian in the field of education, says that "it is the unanimous testimony of historians that for the first two centuries, and for a large part of the third, the life upheld by the Christian Church, with its purity yet unsullied and its ambitions yet untainted, furnished one of the most remarkable phenomena in history; and that this purity of life was largely responsible for the rapidity and thoroughness of its conquest of the Roman world."   Monroe is more specific: "The gladiatorial shows, which had extended their demoralizing influence throughout the Empire, were put down by the Church, though not without a long struggle; divorce, which had become such an evil that it was said men changed their wives as easily as their clothes, was forbidden or strictly regulated; infanticide, which was universally practiced and had been largely responsible for the shrinkage of population and had been combated, when at all, by philosophers and government only on political grounds and hence ineffectively, was now opposed on moral grounds and rooted out of the Church and finally out of society at large; in a similar manner, the exposure of children was definitely treated as murder, and through the teaching of the early Church and the large sums of money which it spent for the care of such children, was discontinued; the immoral ceremonies and the lascivious practices of private worship in the pagan religions were of course denied all the communicants of the new Church and were in due time driven from public tolerance.   In these respects and, above all, through the high standards of personal morality, as expressed in the Mosaic Law and the Sermon on the Mount, standards altogether unknown among the masses of the population, the early Church enforced a moral education that was entirely new in the history of the world and the history of education. If one will compare the simplicity and purity of the character of early Christian worship with the ceremonies of the pagan religions; the character of the Christian priesthood with that of the pagan cults; the morality inculcated in the one with the habit fostered in the other; the sacrifice entailed in the one with the indulgence granted in the other; the humanitarian sentiments in the one with the cruelty and brutality, however refined, in the other; the charity and generosity of the one with the selfishness of the other; if these comparisons be made, the importance of Christian education will be readily understood."

This brief and inadequate survey is sufficient to establish the fact that a full-orbed Christian education is a medium through which God can effect the redemption of mankind today. The unchanging basic elements of human nature and of divine truth, if properly integrated and developed by capable teachers, may form the basis for building a new and better world.

The Apostolic era was a demonstration ground upon which it was proven that the local church should be primarily responsible for the Christian education of the masses and that every disciple of Christ, from ministers and teachers through the entire lay membership of the Church, should accept a definite responsibility in the educational process.

The early Church accepted its educational task and discharged its obligation with complete dedication motivated by the conviction that Christ was coming soon. It was spurred by the imperative that men must be taught and saved ere it was too late to teach and save at all. It was a case of *teach or perish!* The results of their labors speak volumes for the inspiration and guidance of our modern Christian leaders as they would develop an effective educational strategy for the times.

Chapter VII

TEACH OR PERISH

THE last best hope of the Church, the nation and the world lies in Christian education — in an immediate, comprehensive, universal, mass program of Christian education at the local church and community level.

H. G. Wells, the noted English novelist and historian, said, shortly before his death, "The salvation of Western civilization depends on the outcome of a race between education and catastrophe." He is not alone among responsible thinkers and observers in this view. If he had said "Christian education" he would have been nearer the truth.

It is not unthinkable that total collapse may overtake our civilization. Certain somber facts are emerging, solid and inexorable.

The world has tried *science* as a human panacea for its ills. Science has contributed many discoveries and inventions which have vastly advanced our civilization materially, but science in the hands of evil men and evil forces is a threat to human survival.

The world has tried *social reform,* with resulting amelioration of much human suffering and frustration, but efforts to reconstruct society have raised more problems than they have solved.

The world has tried *international agreement,* with consequent broadening of understanding and ideals in world affairs, but most of them have become mere scraps of paper in the absence of moral responsibility.

The world has tried new *educational philosophies and techniques,* and these have done much to reduce illiteracy and elevate cultural standards, but education without Christ has increased the cleverness of criminals and created false security in the self-sufficiency of human wisdom.

The world has tried *industrial organization,* increasing efficiency and raising the economic status of the worker. It has enabled management and labor to settle their problems by means of collective bargaining. But there is still selfish, bitter warfare between both camps.

The world has tried *big government* and has achieved massive social and political results, but centralization of authority and power has resulted in losses of individual freedom and dangers of revolution.

While the masses eat, drink and make merry, there is a widespread weakening of fundamental wisdom and virtue. There is intellectual confusion, social unrest and uncertainty of purpose. The achievements of men, marvelous and glorious as they seem, have only led the world up a blind alley. For the first time in history the tools for the total extermination of mankind are in its hands. As Winston Churchill puts it, "Death stands at attention, obedient, expectant and ready to serve . . . ready to pulverize without hope of repair, what is left of civilization." Coupled with this stark fact is the teaching of the prophetic Word of God that man's history must inevitably end in man's judgment before the awful throne of God.

Yet, despite this "background of black," the world does not have to perish now. If it does, it will be because there are no longer the proverbial "ten righteous men" through whom God can work.

There are glimmerings of hope in the attitude of millions who have been disillusioned about the sufficiency of scientific and technological achievement and who feel that mankind's hope lies in a Power outside and above this world. More men will talk about religion today than in many a long year. They are beginning to realize that man is not naturally good, that he is diseased at the root of his being, that even his best intentions are frustrated from within.   Dr. Pitirim A. Sorokin of Harvard said recently, "The more we study man, his conduct and psychology, the stronger grows the conviction that he in no wise resembles the 'good little boy' that the eighteenth century and the modern rationalism depict. . . . Before us we have not only a sensible being, but the elemental man, who is not only peace-loving, altruistic, compassionate, but also full of rancor, cruelty, bestiality; not only consciously clear-sighted, but often blind; not only gentle and creative, but wild and destructive. . . . The quantity and quality of man's impulses and reflexes render him, singularly, like a bomb full of different kinds of forces and tendencies capable of bursting and presenting us with a picture of wild disorder." In a society which is beginning to recognize its shortcomings and is growingly hungry for moral and spiritual help, a society which is clamoring for a new certainty of mind and a better way of life, there is ground for a new Christian educational offensive.

Such an offensive could not only result in redeemed men but it could give democracy a new lease on life, with a foundation upon the sovereignty of God, His law, His will and His providential leading.   It could give a true purpose to liberty and furnish the moral and spiritual disciplines by which liberty can be maintained and perpetuated.   It could condition the minds of free men with the principles and the faith which can face the challenge of materialistic ideologies and totalitarian governments.   America must either learn anew this way of life and practice it or she will perish.

Not only is the nation threatened with total collapse but so is Christianity, as this modern generation has known it.   This is no plea to preserve and perpetuate the traditions and establishments which are the constructs of fallible religious leaders and which are foreign in spirit and character to the Church that Jesus and His Apostles built.   It is well that Christianity is being tried as by fire in the crucible of crisis.   Its drosses need to be consumed and destroyed.   The world must see, through the great ecclesiastical establishments, magnificent temples and cathedrals, the huge endowments, dramatic liturgies and political and social prestige, to the real *body of Christ* of which He is the Head. Too often the modern Church has lost its common touch with men and has failed to convey the Gospel message which it was created to teach and live. Too often it does not have the courage to deal effectively with the forces of evil which threaten to destroy the world. This assertion, that the Church is threatened with collapse, is to say that it may well be facing another dark age, comparable to that which engulfed it in Medieval times prior to A.D. 1500. In that day the Church as an institution was so closely linked with the State and other secular forces then undergoing inevitable change, and was so weakened by the ignorance of its constituency, its superstitions and moral poverty, that it completely failed in its divine mission. Taking refuge in the isolation of its monasteries and in its ecclesiastical fortress in Rome it eked out a miserable existence until the Reformation restored true Christianity to life. During these terrible years there was grave doubt whether Christianity would ever regain its lost ground and be perpetuated as a great religion. While the causes for the present retreat of Christianity may not be exactly similar, there are startling and fearful identities which should cause Christians to pause and ask themselves whether history might not repeat itself. It is true that Christ said, "On this rock I will build my church and the gates of hell shall not prevail against it," but He did not promise that it would never have to pass through the "valley of the shadow of death."

God is not dead. The living Christ is still here. The power of the Holy Spirit is still available in full measure. The resources of heaven are sufficient to enable fully committed Christians to initiate a new educational crusade fully adequate for the times. It is possible for men to catch a new moral vision and to have the courage to live by that vision. God can kindle in the sluggish and indifferent a new zeal for truth and an aggressive antagonism to error wherever it may exist. He can give a confidence in the ultimate triumph of truth. He can give strength to attempt the seemingly impossible and to accomplish it in His name. He can keep the central and eternal things clear amid the secondary concerns that clamor for attention. He can keep dedicated Christians moving toward His high goals even when they cannot go another inch in their own strength.

⌞The Church today, with all its weaknesses and shortcomings, is far stronger today than it was in the days of the Caesars, or in the days of the Dark Ages. It has millions more capable and consecrated disciples of Christ, it has more material resources, it has outposts farther out on the rim of Christendom. There is no reason, except ignorance of the true faith and lack of faith in God, to keep her from again "turning the world upside down."⌟

Let us dwell for a moment on this matter of "ignorance of the true faith." If Christian education is the hope of the Church, of the nation and of the world, what of its nature and content? There must be no misunderstanding or doubt here.

The Christian education adequate for the times must be positively and constructively doctrinal. Life is founded on belief. "As a man thinketh in his heart, so is he." One of the weaknesses of modern Christian education is its pragmatic skepticism which rejects the Bible as the central and normative source of divine truth. The apostolic Church recognized certain fundamental and immutable Christian teachings concerning the person, nature and mission of Christ and concerning the way in which all men must walk if they are to enjoy eternal life. The early Church presented the Christ who died for our sins according to the Scriptures, who was buried and rose again according to the Scriptures and who lives eternally as the only hope of the sinner. Apostolic teaching included doctrines about God, man, sin, salvation, righteousness and the ultimate end of man. It is perfectly clear that this strangely powerful Christian movement emerged from comparative obscurity in a backward land to challenge the religions and philosophies, the cultures and the powers of the times with beliefs and convictions capable of changing and transforming mankind. It tolerated no theological theories of the fatherhood of God and the brotherhood of man based on the essential goodness of man. It demanded absolute surrender to Christ the Way, the Truth and the Life.

This is no time for compromise. The Church cannot afford to take the soft approach to systems of thought and codes of conduct which are manifestly inimical to the highest good of man and hostile to the revealed truth of the Holy Scriptures. The Church has gone too far in seeking to accommodate its thought and its modes of thinking to those of the modern world. Christian truth is revealed from God, is savingly different and produces a unique society. Christian education for the times must make these distinctions crystal clear so that all men may see. This may make the Church less popular, but it will make it more powerful and productive.

Christian education for today and tomorrow must be positively and constructively intolerant of evil. It needs to spell out in no uncertain terms the way of death and in juxtaposition to it the way of life. It must boldly condemn error in all its forms. It must lovingly and helpfully train men to exemplify the characteristics of the good life. This calls for no withdrawal from the world but rather for dangerous, challenging living in the midst of evil.

This leads to the corollary principle that Christian education must be positively and constructively ethical. God is holy and in His presence no unclean thing can stand. Christ presented a life of perfect goodness. Christians, while they may not be perfect, stand before God in the merit of Christ their Saviour and are conscious that they have been saved for holiness. They realize that no man can make a high profession of faith and continue in sin without being a hypocrite and bringing reproach upon Christ and the Church. Christians must so live that others seeing their good works will be constrained to follow Christ. It was the startling and convincing difference between the lives of Christians and the lives of others, in the first three centuries of the Christian era, which at once incurred the hatred of evil men and won the admiration of all seekers after the good life. Christian education must inspire and train men to a type of ethical conduct which can undergird and make possible a good society. "If the salt hath lost its savour, wherewith shall it be salted?"

Christian education must positively and constructively express Christianity's love and good-will toward all men. Humanity everywhere must realize that the Church is in the world to minister to the needy, "heal the brokenhearted, deliver the captives, recover sight to the blind, and set at liberty the bruised." Christians must be taught to show love and consideration to men of high and low estate, rich and poor, learned and ignorant, without regard to race or nation. This love will be far too intense a passion of the inner heart to be satisfied with mere expression in philanthropy or social welfare. It will never be content to express itself in gifts of mere creature comforts or in the dissemination of some new social doctrine. It will somehow convey in warm sincerity the loving care of the heavenly Father who sent His only Son into the world, not to condemn the world but to save the world. It will not be content until it has brought the last and least of the lost into the full warmth and joy of the household of faith and somehow impregnated the social order with a new idealism and made the world a better place in which to live.

Christian education for today and tomorrow must completely recapture the characteristics of Christian education in the early Church. It must be primarily a local-church responsibility; it must be a major concern in all the churches; it must be for the whole membership and for as many others outside the communion as can be induced to take instruction; it must be intensely evangelistic; it must be synonymous with life itself and, in close association with the leadership of the Church, it must be responsible for the nurture and discipline of those who look to it for protection and guidance. Because of the extreme exigencies of the hour the Church must through all its local congregations mount this kind of an educational program. It must *teach or perish!*

What are the prospects for such an educational crusade?

Out of some 300,000 congregations in the nation less than one-fourth have anything approximating an efficient and effective church-school program, and even fewer have the spiritual power and evangelistic spirit necessary to accomplish what the world situation would require.

Most Protestant Sunday schools are serving a worthy purpose. In fact, if it were not for them, inadequate as they are, the churches would be almost devoid of biblically intelligent members. But the average schools are plodding along on a treadmill of worn-out tradition and mediocrity, quite unaware of their responsibility to a changing world and of their potentiality in bringing a new and better day. They go along doing the things they have always done, keeping the organizational wheels greased and turning, teaching hit-skip portions of the Bible in a seven-year curricular merry-go-round. They do, it must be said, touch lives with Christian truth, and helpful results ensue; the good these schools do must not for a moment be underestimated. The dedication and earnest endeavor of many of their teachers and leaders should be more widely recognized and appreciated. But the stark and cruel fact is that the traditional American Sunday school is about as far removed from what the Church should be doing educationally as the stagecoach is from jet travel in the field of communications.

One of the many proofs of this inadequacy is to be found in a recent survey conducted by the chaplains in the U.S. armed services. Chaplains are continually amazed at the degree of apathy and ignorance, varied somewhat according to denominational background, which Christian draftees display concerning the Christian faith. Something is decidedly wrong with the system of Christian education which produces so many doctrinal illiterates and such widespread spiritual indifference. Actually, many of these recruits who had declared themselves some brand of Protestant, had never heard of Calvary and could not spell redemption, let alone define it. An astonishing number could not repeat the Lord's Prayer, the Ten Commandments or tell who Abraham, Moses, David, Peter or Paul was. Men and women like this are evidently members of the churches and representative of the frightfully large number of "nominal Christians" who are a dead weight to Christianity. These young people went to Sunday school because their parents insisted. They got poor Bible training. The things they were taught were so irrelevant in the light of what they learned in the secular schools that they were soon discredited and discarded. Participation in colorless social gatherings, "outreach" projects and discussion groups left them with no clear grasp of what real Christianity stands for. Following their friends into church membership like a flock of sheep into a corral, they never fully understood why they took the step. As "wise" adolescents they probably ceased going to Sunday school altogether.

Something of this same situation obtains in both liberal and evangelical churches. In the former it is aggravated by the fact that teachers and leaders hold an extremely rationalistic view of the Bible, the one distinctive authority upon which Protestantism rests. In the latter, sound doctrine has too often been taught in the abstract, with little relationship to daily living. Conservatism, in these churches, has a tendency to settle into a reactionary spirit impervious to progressive educational programs and methods. Too often teachers are incompetent and lesson materials of dubious quality. Bernard Iddings Bell once made the valid criticism: "Protestantism . . . seems . . . to be losing its religious appeal . . . because its pedagogy is so atrocious."

But the educational potential of the average Protestant church in America is tremendous. It has numerous organizations and groups engaged in some form of educational work. It has buildings and equipment capable of accommodating a greatly improved and enlarged program. It has capable personnel either experienced in educational work or with the capacity for training and service. All the resources for advance are simply waiting to be mobilized and given leadership.

The latent capacities of Christian laymen and laywomen in thousands of churches constitute an unmined lode of treasure. One of the most unfortunate trends in modern church life is the erection of a barrier between the professional clergy and the laity. In the early Church all Christians had equal responsibility before God for the advancement of the Kingdom, though each was as-

signed tasks suitable to his abilities. Christ began His educational
crusade with consecrated and well-taught fishermen, tax collectors,
tent makers, soldiers, housewives and widows who put the Kingdom
first in their lives. The Apostles built no wall of separation between their work and that of those they recruited in the churches.
These laymen heard the call, saw the opportunity, accepted the
task and gave themselves sacrificially in daily service. There is
no reason why the whole Church cannot be inspired to duplicate
their example today.

The Sunday school movement itself was founded by a businessman, Robert Raikes. Its greatest leaders since that time, at local,
regional, national and international levels have been laymen. One
of the finest examples of latent talent given freedom to develop
through the Sunday school was Dwight L. Moody. As a rather
unpromising shoe salesman he heard a great Christian leader say,
"The world has yet to see what God can do with just one man
who would give himself completely in His service." Moody was
so stirred that he went to his pastor and offered to teach a Sunday-
school class. The minister was not impressed and expressed regret
that there were no openings for teachers. Then Moody insisted
that if he were given a chance he would build up his own class
out of boys in the community who never darkened the door of a
church. Finally he was assigned to the boiler room of the church
in the hope that his ardor would cool. He filled that room with
boys. When he asked for more space, he was denied it. But still
on fire with consecrated purpose Moody found a saloon which was
closed on Sunday and continued to build his class and lead boys
to accept Christ as Saviour. When that building was outgrown,
he rented an empty store building, recruited helpers and eventually built one of the largest Sunday schools in America. Not every
layman is a Dwight L. Moody, but the potential in the unused
talents of thousands of American church members is tremendous.
And the challenge still stands, "The world has yet to see what
God can do with just one man who would give himself completely to His service."

Today Protestant churches offer an average of fifty hours of religious instruction annually in comparison with three hundred hours offered by Roman Catholic and Jewish schools. Children receive as many as three thousand hours annually of secular instruction, much of which is based on an anti-Christian philosophy. It is apparent that time schedules and curriculum content in Protestant church schools must be vastly expanded. Thousands of new teachers must be recruited and trained. New schools must be planted in untouched areas. A new conviction, zeal and willingness to sacrifice must take possession of Protestant teachers and leaders.

What would happen if Protestant church schools went at their task with the same breadth of vision, depth of commitment and certainty of purpose as that displayed by Communist and Roman Catholic education? These two massive complexes have no doubts about the necessity of education and will not tolerate ignorance in any matters which they consider essential to survival and advance. No sacrifice of time or energy, no expenditure of money or materials is too great if believed essential to the accomplishment of desired ends.

Communism appeals to man's idealism and asks life or death commitment to "the greatest cause in the history of mankind." Communists boast that their vision and courage have never been matched by that of any heroes in the annals of history. They do not doubt the inevitability of their triumph over all their foes. They indoctrinate their leaders with the Party line, they set up goals and a time schedule for their achievement. Failure brings banishment or death.

Teachers in the Roman Catholic educational system have the same complete commitment. Most of them are members of orders which require a life commitment. This involves strict discipline, chastity, poverty and obedience. They have a clear understanding of the fundamentals of the Christian faith as interpreted in Roman Catholic dogma and they are required to implant that faith in such a thorough manner as to guarantee lifetime allegiance of the pupil to the Roman Catholic Church. For centuries the Church failed to realize the necessity for mass education, confin-

ing its chief educational efforts to the development of the priesthood and the *religieuse,* but today its program is broadening to
include all Catholics and as many others as it can influence. Roman Catholics know that they must teach or perish in this changing world and they are doing it.

The necessity for Protestantism to mount a new and thoroughly
adequate educational crusade is imperative. The climate is ripe
for it and the resources are available.

We must *teach* God's Word. . .

We must *teach* the sovereignty of God. . .

We must *teach* God's will and way. . .

We must *teach* the love of God. . .

We must *teach* Christ as Saviour and Lord. . .

We must *teach* the Way of Salvation. . .

We must *teach* the Way of Life. . .

We must *teach* the folly of error. . .

We must *teach* the Christian world-view. . .

We must *teach* fellowship with Christ. . .

We must *teach* love and goodwill toward men. . .

We must *teach* the Gospel of the Kingdom. . .

We must *teach* the certainty of eternal judgment. . .

We must *teach* the inevitability of Christ's triumphant reign. . .

We must *teach* men to observe all things whatsoever Christ
has commanded. . .

We must *teach . . . or perish!*

Chapter VIII

CHRISTIAN EDUCATION FOR THE TIMES

CHRISTIAN education, as it faces its responsibilities in the modern world, must make a high decision. As an institution in American life it faces the dilemma posed by its being in some sense bound up with American culture and being bound to Christ. Christianity in America faces the same dilemma.

To be bound up too closely with a culture which is becoming increasingly pagan would involve Christian education in compromise and disloyalty to Christ and the Christian way of life. The Church cannot settle for an education that is partly secular and partly Christian. Christian education must be unequivocally and absolutely Christian and come to grips with modern life realistically in a Christian perspective.

In previous chapters intimations as to the nature of true Christian education have already been made, but the matter is of such vital importance that it needs to be more thoroughly developed.

Christian education for today and tomorrow must be God based. The Bible, its chief and normative textbook, in its opening sentence lays down the principle, "In the beginning, God. . . ." It asserts, by divine inspiration, that the universe and man are the creation of God and are creatures of His will. In the beginning God Himself instructed man concerning His will for him. Through the ages God has revealed His will through divinely inspired men through the medium of the home, the church and the school. The Bible reveals the characteristics of true religious education (1) as to purpose: To achieve a harmonious relationship between God and man; (2) as to method: Positive and authoritative indoctrination relevant to all of life; and (3) as to ends: The glory of God and the ultimate establishment of His kingdom.

This type of Christian education answers the deepest desires of the human heart and gives satisfying answers to such fundamental questions as: Whence came I and to what purpose? What is the true source of man's hope? What authority should I acknowledge? What basic foundations and values should I accept? What way of life will bring lasting satisfaction and reward? What is the end of man? The answers to these questions are found in the Holy Scriptures and are just as satisfying today as they were 2000 years ago. It is true that they are in anti-position to many popular modern answers, but every pragmatic test has been applied to them through the ages and they still stand justified in the lives of millions.

Christian education must *give the true view of man.* It breaks with the naturalistic view that the *genus homo*, after thousands of years of biological evolution, emerged from his ape ancestry in a state of ignorance; and that, being an observant creature and possessed with the powers of reason and imagination, man came to assume a dominant position in the natural world. According to this view, man's future is problematical but it is likely that death ends all. The educational philosophy built on this hypothesis proceeds on the assumption that the child in its growth simulates the evolutionary development of the race. It takes the sentimental and unrealistic view that the child is innately good, wise and virtuous and that the educational task is to develop his natural powers along moral and spiritual lines of his own choosing. Christian education accepts the biblical view of man, a view with insights unexcelled for their profundity and divine understanding. It sees man as created by God "in his image," but the victim of all the darkness and enmity towards God to which the sins of his forebears have doomed him. Yet it sees him as capable of accepting redemption in Christ and realizing the hopes which God has for him and which he has. Christian education offers man a new birth into the family of God and eternal security in the kingdom of heaven. It places a premium on the individual, helps him toward personal integration and a harmonious relationship with God and a just and noble society.

Christian education must *give a true view of God*. It does this through the presentation of Jesus Christ, the Son of God and Himself very God. Man learns to know what God is like by coming to know and understand Christ, His mission, His teaching and His redeeming and sustaining power. Christian education goes beyond mere philosophical theism. It presents a personal God with a personal interest in human persons and as One to whom man is personally responsible. He is always concerned with the prayer of His children and watches with care every aspect of life. Christian education thus presents no icy intellectual concept of God, but a warmly vital image of Fatherhood and Brotherhood. It establishes a God-man relationship which sustains and gives new meaning to life.

Christian education *must give a true world-view*. It recognizes the universe as the creation of an omnipotent, transcendent and purposeful God. "The heavens declare the glory of God and the firmament showeth his handiwork." He is the author and sustainer of natural law, and man's discoveries in this realm only prove God's eternal provision for the natural welfare of mankind. These laws and the material resources which they control are abundantly adequate to serve all man's physical needs. Scientific inquiry is constantly challenged by the seemingly endless possibilities inherent in His universe. The reverent scientist is humble in the face of them and thankful for God's eternal goodness. History, properly viewed, is a panorama of the conflict of Good and Evil in terms of human behavior. This conflict is overruled by divine providence for man's ultimate good and the final accomplishment of the purposes of God. Eventually, says Christian education, God's Kingdom will come, His will be done, on earth as it is in heaven.

Christian education must *have a true view of culture*. It is not obscurantist. It does not put up fences or set up an *Index Expurgatorius* against the views of science, philosophy, and theology; or against the beauties of literature, music and the classic arts. All the best that has been thought and done by man is considered as a challenge to high achievements employing all the resources and talents of man. Such an education does, however, maintain a high moral and spiritual standard of evaluation and use. As the Apostle Paul put it, "Whatsoever things are true, whatsoever things are lovely, whatsoever things are of good report; if there be any virtue and if there be any praise, think on these things." Christian education should always provide the fullest possible expression of the highest and best that is within man through all the talents and skills with which he is endowed.

Christian education for the times will *involve evangelism*. Personal commitment to Christ as Saviour and Lord is essential if the pupil is to be a true disciple. This commitment will embrace a change in personality, habits, purposes, attitudes, motives and character traits. A whole series of decisions must follow "the great decision" and "the born-again experience." Each teacher and leader should know the joy of salvation in his own life, have a passion for lost souls, be soundly instructed in the Holy Scriptures, and keep himself unspotted from the world. Thus his wisdom and judgment will be respected and his appeals for life commitment will be effective. Each class should be so imbued with the spirit of evangelism that it will constantly recruit new disciples and encourage growing Christians in the attainment of "the more abundant life" in Christ.

The importance of *indoctrination* has already been mentioned, but so important is this phase of Christian education that it will bear additional emphasis. If the pupil is to do God's will, he must know God's will. God's will is to be found in God's Word. The Bible, therefore, must not only have a central place in the curriculum, but it must control and modify all textbooks and teaching. It must be the standard by which the pupil measures and evaluates what is taught. Every pupil should be thoroughly in-

doctrinated in Bible truth, should memorize its fundamental teachings and its most inspiring passages, learn how to use it as a
guide to daily living and as a means of instructing others in the
way of salvation and the good life. The man who would be
"thoroughly furnished unto every good work" should know the
whole Bible — its history, its laws, its devotional materials, its
theology, its ethics, its prophecies — in their proper dispensations
of God's grace and in their relevance to modern life. Courses in
the origins and histories of the Bible books and in the modern use of
the Bible are essential if intelligent people are to put their faith
in it as a trustworthy guide. Worthy new translations and versions should be examined for new light on eternal truth. The
Bible is not to be considered as a fetish or as a ouijaboard for
strange divinations. It must be subject to reasonable laws of interpretation and human understanding. This lays a heavy responsibility upon teachers as interpreters of sacred truth in a modern and often hostile world. But without the Bible there is no
such thing as Christian education or knowing the will of God.

Christian education involves *experimentation* and *demonstration.* If Christianity is to be something more than mere commitment to abstract doctrine, denominational distinctives and organizational loyalties; if it is to be something meaningful, vital and
challenging in the lives of individuals and society, Christianity
must be experienced and demonstrated. It is precisely at this
point that much so-called Christian education has failed. In
secular education, for example, the principle of physics is taught
in the classroom and such instruction is followed by laboratory ex-
periments which demonstrate the validity of the principles of
physics. The pupil is inspired to go on in advanced study and
experiment and to utilize his knowledge in some business or profession. Why should not the validity of Christianity be scientifically demonstrated in the laboratory of life? Learning God's
will should be definitely related to doing God's will. In a very
real sense Christian education is a school of life. Typical conduct
situations may well be proposed in which Bible truth is applied.
They will involve personal dedication, clarity of purpose, surren-

der of inherited impulses, submission to divine authority, and a sincere desire to achieve a good end to the glory of God. The pupil should learn how to live a Christian life in all sorts of situations. Christian education may well provide as a part of its curricular activities participation in relief and welfare projects, service in the solution of community problems and constructive contributions in public affairs. It is important that all such projects be controlled and directed as a part of the educational process and evaluated for their relevance to Christian responsibility.

Christian education involves *nurture*. The church school should be a nursery and a hospital for moral and spiritual growth and health. Beginning with the child, each life should be cherished, fostered, fed and disciplined. Growth can be measured in terms of attendance, punctuality, Bible reading, giving, study, prayer, participation and good works. In the crucial adolescent years there is imperative need for personal and group counselling dealing with every phase of the pupil's life. Problems arising from physical and psychological change and from conflict with worldly philosophies and social mores are especially critical. Choices are made that can change the whole course of life. It is a tragic fact that hundreds of thousands of youth are lost to the Church because of the apathy or ignorance of church-school teachers who are supposed to be responsible for the nurture of youth. It is too often assumed that when the pupil reaches "the age of accountability" he is no longer in need of nurture. No human being ever gets beyond that need. The school should provide confessional counselling and Christian psychological clinics to deal with extreme cases. When there are instances of sinful conduct, the first duty of teachers and class leaders is to offer their help in the spirit of Christian love and compassion, while at the same time they make clear the need for repentance, restitution and recovery. Spiritual curative care of this sort would do much to demonstrate the practical values of Christian education. The pupil nurtured from kindergarten to maturity in communion with Christ, devotion to God's Word, loyalty to the Church and daily Christian living will

grow up into that full stature and fullness of Christ which is the
end of Christian education.

The teacher is the key figure in effective Christian education.
The kind of teaching and the type of teacher will determine the
degree of effectiveness. Children, youth and adults require specialized teaching approach and procedure. This presupposes specialized training. Ideally, at least three years should be devoted
to basic study. The last two years should be accompanied by
practice teaching. Bible knowledge is foundational. There should
be studies in the Four Gospels, the Epistles, Old Testament Law
and History, Old Testament Poetry and Wisdom Literature, Old
Testament Prophecy, New Testament Prophecy, Biblical Theology and Christian Ethics. Beyond the study of the Bible will be
such essential studies as Christian Psychology, Christian Pedagogy,
Christian Nurture, Church History, Christian Theology and a
general survey of Christian Education in the Local Church. De-
partmental specialization courses will be necessary to orient basic
studies to the particular age group to be served. It is obvious that
this is an ideal leadership training curriculum. It cannot be immediately provided in most churches. It can be broadly approxi-
mated in elementary texts, a number of which are available. But
the teacher should never be satisfied until he is intellectually well
equipped for his task.

Teachers should have a clear understanding of the principles
of Christian pedagogy but at the same time be alert to modern
teaching methods. The whole modern communications situation
is in a state of flux, with new discoveries in media and techniques
constantly being made. While many methods in so-called "progressive education" are the result of naturalistic postulates, there
are many that can be used or adapted for use in church schools.
The best possible use should be made of all forms of visual education, group dynamics, the case method, dramatics, discussion
drama, cram courses, outdoor education, music and worship. In
audio-visual education alone there are film strips, motion pictures,
projectroscopes, recording devices, television, religious art exhibi-
tions, radio and other forms of media. Great care should be taken,

however, that the medium does not obscure the teaching aim. In fact, modern teaching methods should never become so obvious and intriguing that they dominate the teaching situation or minimize the communication of subject matter. Neither should they be used to the neglect of personal teaching values and individual personal response.

All teaching methods must be in accord with the purposes of Christ, the Master Teacher. They should conform to the basic educational pattern of the early Church. They should be in harmony with the Spirit of Christ. They should encourage and make more effective the Christian witness in the life of the Church and community.

It is impossible within the confines of one chapter to deal with all the factors involved in the task of Christian education at the local church level. Indeed, that is not the purpose of this work. Texts have been written which provide all the essential details concerning organization, administration, curriculum, building and equipment, and other phases of a well-rounded program. Possibly all factors need to be re-examined in the light of the crucial situation confronting the Church in the modern world. Readjustments and revolutionary changes may need to be made. It is the author's purpose to present only in broad outline the kind of Christian education needed if the local church is to function effectively in this area in these crucial times.

Chapter IX

A NEW COMMITMENT

MOTIVATION for action determines the pattern, the direction and the dynamism of any undertaking. If a young man's commitment to Christ causes him to choose the Christian ministry as his life work, his intention will influence the choice of his friends, the educational institutions he will attend, the choice of a wife and the way he spends his time. The measure of his commitment will largely determine the power of his life. If he can couple his learning, his natural abilities and work patterns with an intense enthusiasm and a consciousness of divine partnership and empowerment, he will go far toward being a succecssful minister. What is true of the individual is also true of movements and institutions. The dominant purpose and devotion determine ultimate accomplishment.

The Christian education movement for today and tomorrow must consist of more than a sound philosophy, a comprehensive curriculum, a trained leadership, effective teaching methods, efficient administration and adequate buildings and equipment. Such resources, as important as they are, without complete commitment to Christ on the part of every person involved will never "get off the ground."

The motivation for Christian education lies in faith in Jesus Christ, the Son of God and the Saviour of the world. There can be no valid Christian motivation of any kind for any purpose apart from faith in Him, personal commitment to Him and to His will as revealed in the Holy Scriptures. The primary weakness of professional Christian education leadership today is due to a woeful lack of such motivation.

Some years ago the superintendent of the Sunday scchool in a large West Coast church was accosted one Sunday morning in one of the halls of its education building by a little slip of a girl who bluntly asked him, "Mister, are you saved?" She had come from a pietistic family that had recently moved "across the tracks" into this better suburban community. They had formerly attended a little chapel where this greeting was a stock approach to strangers. The superintendent was momentarily shocked and answered, "Yes, yes, of course." But that afternoon as he sat meditating in his library, the incident bothered him. The implications of the question caused him to examine himself anew and led him to take new vows of deeper consecration to Christ. Then he began a spiritual survey of the leadership personnel of his school. So stirred was he that he called a special meeting of teachers and officers, related the incident, shared with them his own new-born consecration and challenged them to new commitment. Before the meeting ended, all of them were on their knees in prayer. As the result of this experience there came a new and better day in the life of the school and of the whole church.

This sort of consecration to Christ should characterize the leadership of any new Christian education movement worthy of the name. Every leader, teacher and worker should be a church member in good standing and intelligently equipped, but he should also have had a spiritual confrontation with the living Christ in which he has committed himself body, mind and spirit, intellect, emotions and will to the Lord of life. In this experience Christ will become the primary motive in Christian education. The divine will, as learned from the Holy Spirit through the Scriptures, will then always control the secondary motives and the program itself. Everything which is said or done will thus come to occupy a definable place within a distinctly Christian perspective. When clashes come between the Christian way and other ways, between Christian truth and other ideas, Christ will cast the deciding vote. If this commitment is complete and the human-divine relationship becomes well established, Christ's rulership will become as natural as life itself. Christian education under such auspices is bound to have God's sanction and inspiration.

Christ, the Master Teacher, made this complete and unwithholding commitment the very heart of His earthly educational ministry. His requirements for discipleship were so high that only a comparatively few could qualify. In striking contrast with the capabilities and legal righteousness of the Rich Young Ruler (Luke 18:18-30) He accepted the complete consecration of His disciples who had left houses, parents, brethren, wives, children "for the kingdom of God's sake." Theirs was a commitment of all that they had and all that they were. Theirs was the complete renunciation of the world, the flesh and the devil. Yet in the strange alchemy of this commitment experience, they were conscious of an endowment of "manifold more in this present time, and in the world to come eternal life."

The leadership training Christ required in His school went beyond understanding of the Hebrew Scriptures into the acquirement of Christlikeness. His associates kept intimately in touch with Him. They patterned their lives after His, showing the world that they had been with Jesus and learned of Him. After He ascended into heaven, they received His presence through the Holy Spirit. It was through Him that they received the strength to cope with temptation and trial and to go on to victory in all things that were according to the divine will. Like Paul, the modern disciple of Christ should be able to say, "I am persuaded that neither death, nor life, nor angels, nor principalities, nor things present, nor things to come, nor powers, nor height, nor depth, nor any other creature, shall be able to separate us from the love of God which is in Jesus Christ our Lord." As a fully committed discipleship made possible the miraculous triumph of Christianity in the early centuries of its existence, so only a fully committed discipleship can make its triumph possible today.

Faithful discipleship insures a rewarding partnership in the task of Christian education. The early disciples were conscious that they were "laborers together with God." Teachers in the early Church had a conviction that Christ Himself was concerned about Christian education. Such an awareness of divine concern lent a new dignity and importance to the educational task. They could recall that almost the last words of Christ, the Great Commission, had laid upon the Church the imperative necessity of teaching accompanied with the promise, "Lo, I am with you always. . . ." This divine pledge of partnership sparked a divine enthusiasm for the educational task which should still be evident among Christian educators today. The holy love of God for mankind should encourage belief that heaven will spare no resource of divine affection to break down man's alienation and establish him in righteousness.

Partnership with Christ in the task of Christian education can only be made real when its aims and goals are His. Much of modern religious education which has proven so futile is built around man and the false assumption that human nature is altogether good. It is essentially naturalistic and humanistic in its ideology. Its goal is to help the student discover himself and to develop his personality in a religious atmosphere. This idea of self-expression can as well eventuate in evil as in good. Christian education is built around Christ and has for its aim the perfection of man's nature and a life of complete harmony with God. It is engaged in teaching men the will of God and showing them how to relate themselves to Him so as to receive His divine power and guidance in "the more abundant life." A God-oriented education does not shackle the student. It enlists all his faculties and encourages him to strive for the highest and best and provides him with a Helper and Friend in his struggle.

A Christ-centered educational program involves a thorough commitment to divine truth. Christ accepted the principle of the divine revelation of truth. He spoke words of truth. He approved the Holy Scriptures of His day, "Saying they are they which testify of me." He promised further revelation of divine truth through

His apostles and holy men speaking as the Holy Spirit gave them utterance. This truth is available to us in our New Testament. Thus the Christ-committed school will teach the Bible as the Word of God — divinely inspired and authoritative. It has universal appeal and meets every moral and spiritual need of the human heart. But truth will not be taught for truth's sake alone. It will be used for the well-being of the student. When truth is taught in the abstract it cannot be worthwhile. It must be made to live, in its solutions of the human predicament, in its guidance in moral concerns and in its inspirations to noble living. Christ Himself is the embodiment, the incarnation of truth. The student can see truth in Him. The personality embodying the truth, more often than the abstract truth, is the strategic factor in obtaining acceptance of truth and securing wholehearted commitment to the Christian cause. Carrying this principle a step further, the Christian teacher who reflects in his own life the characteristics of Christ in thought, in speech, in spirit and in conduct, is himself convincing proof of the validity of his teaching.

The Christ-committed teacher will have as his supreme desire the winning of the pupil to Christ and leading him into a personal experience with Him as Saviour and Lord. Man is not only body and mind; he is spirit. His mind is not only intellect; it is also emotions and will. The use that is made of truth is largely determined in the realm of the emotions. In the throes of some deep spiritual experience which may not be directly and immediately related to intellectual knowledge, great decisions are made which motivate life. Christian education builds up to a crisis. This crisis involves the pupil's commitment to Jesus Christ as Saviour and Lord, his repentance, his obedience and his infilling by the Holy Spirit. If this experience is real it produces a regenerated and reborn person — a new creature in Christ. After this experience the things a person once loved, he now hates and the things he once hated, he now loves. Through the gift of the Holy Spirit which is promised to the converted, he is divinely aided to grow in grace and in the knowledge of the truth. This indwelling Presence guides the life; imparts Christian love, joy and peace; helps in infirmity; gives inner strength and enlightens the whole being. Without God the "perfect man" is unattainable; with God all things are possible. This language is foolishness to those who are not Christians. Even to nominal Christians it is only reminiscent of something they may have once read in the Bible or heard in a service of worship. Yet this language is the language of the early Church and of the New Testament. Paul's epistles are replete with it. Unless it is restored to common parlance and in Christian living in the Church of today and to morrow, there is little hope that the Church will again be the power for righteousness that God intended it to be.

Christian educators who are Christ-committed will work untiringly and sacrificially as Jesus worked. As a child He was deeply convicted that He "must be about His Father's business." He never lost that conviction. He was constantly teaching, ministering, healing and serving. He gave His last full measure of devotion on the Cross. In a Christ-centered program of Christian education every teacher and worker should see his task as a divine mission, something to which he can give his whole heart, with ever enlarging opportunities for expression and service. He should go to his work as one would go to worship, with a prayer of thankfulness for the privilege of work and with an aspiration to give the utmost for the highest. There is healing and joy in such work. It will be an expression of the highest and best in his faith and ideals; a realization of man's desire to create, to build and to help; a confirmation of the fact that man was born to bring glory to God and to be a partner in the achievement of His divine purposes.

Constant touch with the living Christ will keep contact with the sources of power so essential in an effective Christian educational program. Prayer is the channel of blessing. Alexis Carrell, the scientist whose dramatic discoveries startled the world, once said, "The most powerful form of energy is available through prayer. When we pray we link ourselves with the inexhaustible motive power that binds the universe. . . . True prayer . . . is a binding necessity in the lives of men and nations." After an hour on one's knees new energy and motive power, new optimism and new spirit to achieve will impregnate the whole being. Collective prayer in which chosen groups, committees, boards, whole classes and departments participate will often be the means of achieving the impossible. When everything seems to be going at cross purposes and there is friction among leaders and people, prayer will bring unity of spirit and action. Prayer will lift horizons, helping small churches to see beyond their limitations and great churches to get world visions of service. Prayer will give a new sense of mission and faith for the future. It will be discovered that more things are wrought by prayer than by the wisdom and strategy of men. In prayer and in personal confrontation with the living Christ, discipleship and partnership will take on a deeper and more vital meaning.

More than anything else, Christian education in our times needs this new commitment to Christ, His will and His way. What would happen if thousands of leaders, teachers and workers would experience, through personal contact with their Lord, a new infilling of His spirit, a new power, a new will and a new impulse to action? "I would fain be to the Eternal God, what one's own hand is to one's self," wrote the nameless author of *Theologica Germanica*. Men who would lead a great new educational crusade must live so close to Christ that their lives always and in all ways respond to the purposes of His Spirit. They must learn to say, as Christ did in the garden of Gethsemane, "Not my will, but thine be done."

Chapter X

AN EXPANDED PROGRAM

CHRISTIAN education at the local church level must be vastly expanded if it is to meet the needs of the hour. Revolutionary changes must take place in the existing order of things. It will be the purpose of this chapter to chart this transformation in broad terms, particularly in the fields of organization and curriculum.

Each local church has peculiar problems involving size, tradition, status, agencies, controls, leadership personnel, building facilities, financial limitations and other circumstances which may modify or eliminate suggestions which will be made. Each church must solve its particular problems in its own way, but approximate the proposed pattern as fully as possible.

It should be assumed that every person and educational organization in the church is in spirit and life committed to the task of communicating the Christian faith, encouraging its practice and making it a dynamic factor in the life of the community. It should also be assumed that all are loyal disciples of Christ and earnestly seeking to discover ever-enlarging opportunities of service.

When the individuals and groups in the church have been "sold" on the necessity for an expanded and reoriented program of Christian education it is reasonable to suppose that they will be ready to make whatever sacrifices might be entailed to undertake it and make it a success. The selling job must be done by a hard core of leadership, a group of kindred spirits, who have seen the vision and have carefully developed a tentative plan which can be put in operation. If possible, this group should include the pastor and key persons in the church staff, church board and educational organizations. Their proposals should be born out of days of prayer, deep spiritual conviction and renewed commitment to Christ and the Church.

A survey of the educational resources of the church in personnel and organization will reveal encouraging potentials. Few churches are using their resources to the fullest possible degree. Unused talent will be discovered which can supply leadership in the enlarged program. Organizations not usually classified as "educational" will offer unusual opportunities for new study groups. Survey information may well be classified in the graded categories usually employed by church schools: Children, Youth, Young Adults and Older Adults.

The *Sunday school, Bible school* or *Church school,* with its classes embracing all age groups and usually meeting on Sunday morning, will be foremost in importance. Its graded curriculum grounded in the Bible text will need to be examined to see whether it provides a comprehensive and theologically trustworthy knowledge of Christian doctrine. Its enrollment should be compared with the church membership rolls to determine whether every member is receiving instruction. Its leadership and program should be evaluated to determine whether better planning, better performance of accepted duties, better trained and more responsible workers, higher goals and more aggressive activity might improve its effectiveness.

Youth groups, probably meeting on Sunday evening, have a tremendous potential. Too often they have no direct connection with the central educational program of the church. Their programs may overlap what is being taught and done in the Youth Division of the Sunday school. Often these group meetings are haphazard, insipid and unworthy of modern youth. Loyalties are often to outside organizations rather than to the local church itself. Classes and projects meaningfully related to modern life may well be introduced. Counselling by consecrated, capable, and personable young adult leadership should be provided.

There is usually a wide variety of *children's agencies* represented in the average church. Foremost are Boy Scouts, Girl Scouts, Camp Fire Girls and Y-Clubs. To these may be added kindergartens, nurseries and junior mission bands. All have laudable purposes and offer opportunities for supplementary educational activities. For instance, the Boy Scouts offer a God and Country Award which involves instruction in the doctrinal position of the church and its general activities. Bible quizzes, Bible memory work, Bible reading projects and catechetical instruction can be introduced and integrated with the church's educational program.

Women of the church have *missionary societies, ladies' aid societies, women's fellowships, circles, guilds, clubs* and other organizations which may well lend themselves to studies which will make their members more intelligent and effective Christians. The educational potential of such groups is often overlooked.

What has been said of the women of the church may also be true of the men. They have *men's brotherhoods, clubs, fellowships* and *discussion groups.* New purpose can be given these organizations if they can be made to feel that they are a part of a program that is "going somewhere." Their concern for the state of the society often lacks practical and purposeful guidance. Bible study strongly oriented to problems of daily living will be welcomed by such groups.

Many local churches now maintain *camps* where church groups of all ages go for *retreats* and *conferences.* Special educational projects for such affairs can be suggested and integrated with the expanded program.

Vacation church schools offer tremendous opportunities. They take advantage of summer vacations and set up educational programs covering two- and three-week periods. It is said that a child will receive as much biblical instruction in one of these schools as in his Sunday-school class in an entire year. The work of these schools should be examined to discover whether it overlaps and duplicates other instruction. The possibility of having more than one session in summer should be examined. Classes may well be provided for young people and adults and evening hours utilized in addition to the customary morning periods. When properly integrated with the central program of instruction these special schools may well provide important supplemental knowledge and guidance.

In somewhat the same category are *week-end* or *Saturday schools, weekday schools, released-time schools* which some churches provide for public school pupils at convenient times. It is important that the teaching staff of the Sunday school know which children are enrolled in these schools and what they are being taught. Supplemental time should be employed for supplemental teaching in supplemental curriculum.

Sunday-evening classes and *week-night classes* are to be found in some churches. It is in this area that the greatest possibilities for an expanded educational program may be found. It is amazing how many church edifices in America are dark on Sunday night. The proverbial vesper service or evangelistic service has about disappeared in metropolitan areas. Where they persist the attendance is small and is composed of "the faithful." In many churches the only evening activity is the youth meeting.

Southern Baptist churches have demonstrated what can be done on Sunday evening. Their Baptist Training Union offers graded instruction in evangelism, stewardship, church history and a wide range of functional studies. Attendance in some churches is almost as large as in the morning Sunday school. The program is largely denominational in character and it produces a church membership that is well indoctrinated in Baptist distinctives. The BTU may well be responsible for much of the amazing growth of this denomination.

The other nights of the week are rather fully occupied in the highly organized church. There is a welter of class and committee meetings, board meetings, social affairs and special church events. However, there is seldom a night in which the whole church membership is involved or all the facilities of the church building are in use. Many of the routine meetings are held merely to "keep the machinery greased and running." The traditional *mid-week meeting* for prayer and instruction has about disappeared. It is possible to develop a night school which offers a wide range of studies for at least five nights a week. Each class could meet for one night only but there could be several classes a week.

The *Christian home* should not be forgotten in this survey. The early Hebrews placed tremendous emphasis on the home as the primary medium of religious instruction. In early American history the Christian home was considered responsible for teaching its children "letters, the catechism and the capital laws of the country." It is possible so to relate the home to the new educational program that it will supplement the work being done in church classes. The enlistment of millions of parents in the training of their children in the way they should go would do more to stop juvenile delinquency and redeem the social order than any similar undertaking. The home can also be a center to which friends and neighbors can be invited for conversations and short-term studies definitely connected with the church's central educational program.

When all the information concerning the various kinds of educational work being done in the church is compiled and consolidated it will be realized that hundreds of hours a year are involved, but it will also be apparent that there is an immense amount of duplication and disorder. Groups committed to laudable objectives are nevertheless working at cross purposes and failing to meet unitedly, comprehensively and effectively the needs of this crisis hour. The survey will also reveal the great potential for expansion.

Somehow the imperative necessity for decisive action must be made clear to the whole church. The *teach or perish* idea must grip the hearts of the people and stir them. Incentives to action must be so impelling that tradition, old loyalties and pride of leadership will be overcome in a deep-seated desire to undertake greater things for Christ and the Church. Where resistance is encountered there should be no hesitancy about creating new channels of study and action. The movement must go forward. It may have to go over, go under or go around opposition but it must go.

A new, widely representative board or commission should draw up a blueprint of the new educational structure in the light of the facts revealed in the survey. The group should utilize every existing agency, every available talent, every hour of usable time. It should adopt a comprehensive curriculum and see that every phase of it is taught and directed by somebody, somehow, sometime, somewhere. The initiation of the program should not wait on perfection. The greatest peril now is delay. It is already late for the Church to awake and move and it may soon be too late.

Curriculum is a major concern. Its content must be such that it will acquaint the learner with God's will, encourage him to acccept it and show him how to put it into practice. God's will is to be found in God's Word. The Bible, therefore, must not only have the central place in the curriculum, but control and modify all curriculum. The teaching of Christ and the Apostles, the needs and capacities of the pupils will determine the nature of the curriculum. It will be graded to serve all ages.

The comprehensive character of the Holy Scriptures makes them applicable to various forms of study for all age groups. There is an abundance of biographical material. Abraham's foibles, Jacob's deceits, Gideon's idolatry, David's crimes, Peter's denials give opportunity for teaching the consequences of sin. In the life of Christ, man without sin is winsomely portrayed. Nothing is more effective than biographical study in which men see themselves mirrored in the lives of other men. There is historical material dealing with, for instance, the question of national behavior in the story of Israel. In righteousness, the people prosper; in sin, they suffer reverses. Repentance and return to do the will of God are followed by prosperity. Prosperity brings subsequent luxury and laxity of morals. So the cycle of history ran thousands of years ago and so it runs today. The Bible contains devotional material in abundance. Out of the experiences of David comes poetry which expresses universal longings of the human heart. In Job humanity is seen in the furnace of affliction wrestling with the problem of good and evil and coming out victorious through faith in God. Paul and John reveal the spiritual discipline of Christian living. Such studies place the pupil in the wholesome climate of the spiritual world and his soul responds and thrives under them. The Bible is the source book for the best in literature, philosophy, sociology, law and all basic culture of the mind and heart. This sacred library of sixty-six books meets every need of human life.

The special age requirements and capacities of pupils are served by the Word of God. While written by adults to adults, the Bible contains materials easily adapted to all. The inherent needs of the pupil may be stated as spiritual, intellectual, physical and social. Each is reflected in personal relations, church relations, community relations, national relations and world relations. Whatever the life situation, biblical truth can be formed to meet it.

Curriculum building today at the local church level already may follow the graded patterns almost universally accepted in church schools, but the range and number of studies must be greatly expanded.

In the traditional classes meeting on Sunday morning the curriculum pattern should include:

Beginner: God, the Heavenly Father, Nature stories from the Bible, choice Bible sentences, simple stories from the life and teachings of Christ.

Primary: God, the Heavenly Father. God and Jesus Christ. More advanced Bible materials of the type indicated above, memorization of simple Psalms and New Testament verses. Projects in learning and living in God's world.

Junior: Memorization of books and divisions of the Bible and historical and theological outlines. Biographical studies of patriarchs, prophets, kings, Christ and the Apostles. The running story of Revelation. Worship. The Church. Decision for Christ.

Junior High: The story of the Christian Church. Paul's mission. Bible studies in Christian living. World-wide fellowship. Christian missions. Ethical standards.

Senior High: Introduction to Christian theology. Ethical standards. Social problems. The Church and science. Facts about the Bible. The New Testament Church. Renewed consecration and commitment to Christ. Christianity vs. Communism. Christian marriage. Organizational responsibilities.

Young Adults: The history, teaching, organization and life of the New Testament Church. Comparative religions. Home and family problems. Christian responsibilities in society. Leadership training.

Older Adults: Studies in separate books of the Bible. Topical research and study in the whole Bible. A wide range of interpretive studies. Problems in Christian living. All kinds of elective studies. Informal study groups. Leadership training. Organizational responsibilities.

Subjects which lend themselves to three months or more of study in all kinds of youth and adult organizations or in special night or day classes may cover a wide range of interest: Fundamentals of the Christian Faith, Prayer, Evangelism, Church Publicity and Public Relations, Doctrinal Distinctives, Stewardship, Missions, Temperance, Studies in Christian Living, Sex, Courtship and Marriage, The Christian Home and Family, Christian Nurture, Social Ethics, Christian Education, Leadership Training, Church History, Comparative Religions, Christianity vs. Communism, Inter-church Relations, Science and Christianity, Church-State Relations, Christian Principles in Business, Christian Principles in Government, Christian Principles in Labor-Management Relations, Christian Principles in International Relations, Classes in New Testament Books, particularly Romans, Galatians, Ephesians, Colossians, Philippians, I and II Corinthians and a Harmony of the Gospels. Great care should be taken to choose only textbooks which are true to the teachings of the Bible. Better have no study at all than the kind which openly or subtly undermines the very foundations of Christianity itself.

Christian education curriculum moves beyond the use of materials and the acquiring of knowledge, into the realm of expressional activity. It is in doing, based upon sound ideas, that validity is demonstrated and good accomplished. Activity is essential to the educational growth of the pupil. He may give intellectual assent to a doctrine, but he will never fully realize that it is true or that it has pragmatic values until he has experienced it or demonstrated it in everyday life. These expressional activities must be controlled and made a definite part of curriculum. This involves the setting up of projects, the accomplishment of certain ends, co-operation and guidance, discipline, evaluation, criticism and reward. It involves the capacity for sustained effort. It means consecration, organization and unchanging purpose. It means the surrender of inherited impulses and submission to divine authority in order to achieve ideal ends. It means the exercise of will power in ways well pleasing to God. Curriculum projects may include: Personal expression, church-related activity, community activity and state, national and/or international undertakings. There is no limit to the possibilities presented in these various categories for personal and group initiative and inventiveness.

Personal experience of God is primary. The pupil's absolute commitment to Jesus Christ as Lord and Saviour will lead to the conversion experience. He will come to know the reality of the unseen power which is available to him in his work. Through prayer, Bible study and divine guidance this close personal relationship will flower into undying fellowship with Christ. Prayer meetings, testimony meetings and worship services will be helpful in keeping this personal experience alive and operative.

Active participation in the life of the church is important especially in expressional groups. Here the pupil will learn to speak in public, discuss religious and social problems, and think with others about the application of Christian principles to life situations. There will be participation in such practical tasks as visiting the sick, helping the weak and needy, giving guidance to the perplexed and winning men to Christ as Lord and Saviour. In

the modern complex of church organization there will be a temptation to form lesser loyalties and become engaged in routine tasks
which serve no greater purpose than to "make the wheels go
round." This sort of "participation in the life and mission of the
church" should be avoided like poison.

As soon as the pupil becomes a thoroughly committed and experienced Christian he is ready to venture into his ultimate task
of living the Christian life in a darkening world. In his home,
his business or profession and his social relationships he will be
an ambassador of Christ. He should understand that although
he is in the world he is not a part of it to the extent that he is
subject to its philosophy of life, or its accepted customs. In a
humble, Christ-like spirit he will propagate Christian ideas and
demonstrate in his individual character and conduct the superiority of the Christian way of life. The church school may well,
as a part of its curricular activities, encourage pupil participation
in relief projects, social causes, conferences on industrial, educational, governmental and other issues. From the viewpoint of
the school these projects should be considered as educational
processes through which the pupil grows in stature. Suitable recognition of attainment should be provided annually. From the
pupil's viewpoint, he should see himself as Christ's man engaged
in realizing his life purpose and accomplishing the will of God
in society.

With such a comprehensive concept there will be many new
and strange problems to face in building the church school for
today and tomorrow. The central board or committee charged
with this responsibility will need to be constantly in prayer for
wisdom and guidance. They will need to rethink and redesign
carefully what has been done in the past, preserving everything
that is worthwhile, unifying it and integrating it into the new
program. Painstaking work and experimentation will be necessary.
Constant consultation with leaders and workers in all existing
organizations and groups involved will help pave the way for
change and preserve co-operation and good will.

Expansion in new classes and new subjects of study will offer the most thrilling and rewarding part of the new adventure. When the church sees educational activity doubled, trebled or quadrupled, and begins to feel its impact, it will be stirred to new life. New ideas will come from new sources of potential leadership, and the central body should encourage responsible persons to undertake new projects.

Leadership education should get priority as a separate curricular problem. New leaders, carefully trained and imbued with the new ideals and ideas are vital to the success of the new program. The general study courses and the specialized studies should be set up with the demands of church-wide curriculum in mind but not so bound by it that the new leaders will become mere cogs in the machinery. They should be encouraged to acquire an integrity, initiative and creativity of their own which will make for constant and consistent improvement and progress in every phase of the movement.

This somewhat precise and comprehensive pattern set forth in this chapter should not be used as a pretext for setting up some organizational behemoth or for forcing the church into some kind of educational strait jacket. The concern has been more to raise the sights of educational leaders in local churches and give them a vision of "the promised land" that lies ahead. A church is a living organism. Its members are human beings whose spiritual welfare must always have priority over mechanism. The guidance of the Holy Spirit expresses itself in many different ways in various situations. What will work in one church may not work in another. But if this suggested program of expansion can stimulate the magnificent obsession that Christian education and the church school are the hope of the world it will serve its purpose. Above all, the Church world-wide must do something to translate that obsession into something bigger and better than it has ever done educationally. It must *teach or perish!*

Chapter XI

A GROWING IMPERATIVE

THESE changing times are laying a still further educational obligation upon the local church and the Christian community. The American public school, which formerly had an unqualified commitment to religion and morality as basic to the good life, is rapidly becoming secularistic and amoral; indeed, in many places it is antagonistic to the Christian faith and life.

Christian parents and Christian churches owe it to their children to instruct and nurture them in the Christian faith and to protect them from educational forces which would endanger or destroy that faith.

For two thousand years the Church has believed that education is a unitary process which embraces the whole of life and that Christ must be at its center. It has considered itself responsible under God for moral and religious instruction, and while it has admitted the right of the State to teach and train its future citizens in secular matters, it has never admitted the right of the State to undermine and destroy the moral and religious foundations of the Christian community.

In the early history of America education was in the hands of the churches and was distinctly Christian in character. When the unique American public school system was initiated in 1837, in order to unify the American community and undergird Amer-

ican democracy with an intelligent citizenry, religion and morality
were universally accepted as basic to education. Horace Mann,
who is considered "the father of the American public schools,"
strongly advocated this principle. Despite all that his enemies
and detractors did to oppose him, he is on record in scores of
pronouncements, insisting not only on the fundamental educational
importance of religion and morality, but on the necessity of "practical obedience to the precepts of the Gospel of Jesus Christ."
Mann was a churchman. During his later years he became the
first president of Antioch College, founded by the Christian
Churches of Ohio. As leader of the public school movement in
Massachusetts and in the nation, he advocated the reading and
study of the Bible, prayer and "the inculcation of the fundamental
principles of Christianity" in the public schools, although he was
committed to "the separation of Church and State" and opposed
"favoring any particular religious sect" or "converting the schools
into an engine of religious proselytism." So close was the relationship of the early American public schools to the Protestant
churches that atheists, deists and Roman Catholics raised violent
protests concerning bias and bigotry.

In 1840 Roman Catholics in the eastern part of the United
States set up their own parochial schools. In 1884 Middle Western
bishops took similar action. At first they actively opposed public
schools as "Protestant." Today their opposition is grounded on
the amoral and anti-religious character of the schools.

The so-called "Mann Era" was followed by a period in which
the educational philosophy of William Torrey Harris dominated
the American public schools. He was a devoted disciple of Hegel
and favored the separation of religion from public education to
the complete secularization of the process. Harris regarded himself as a Christian and believed that the United States of America
was essentially a "Christian nation," but he conceived of public
education as wholly compartmentalized from religion and as a
distinctly social process. As such it had a morality of its own
which was expressed in certain "social virtues." These included
"all forms of politeness, good-breeding, urbanity, decorum, mod-

esty, respect for public opinion, liberality, magnanimity" and virtues "relating to justice," such as "honesty, fair-dealing with others
respecting the rights of the person, property and reputation" and
"integrity, uprightness and righteousness." Harris was an ex-
tremist in his interpretation of the constitutional principle of the
separation of Church and State, and used it to oppose all "religious
encroachments" on the preserves of the public school. In his
later life Harris held that the thinking cultivated in the schools
should be "hostile and skeptical in its attitude toward religious
truth."

The "Harris Era" was succeeded by the years in which the
philosophy of John Dewey determined public school ideology,
method and program. Naturalistic and scientific in its viewpoint, it had no place for Christian concepts of morality or religion. Dewey described his philosophy as "instrumentalist." He
held that all the gifts of man are instruments of control. Thinking and knowing are instruments by which obstacles are overcome
and the mind set free. Ideas are instruments of integration, con-
tinuity and survival. Education is an instrument by which the
developing and changing child is encouraged on his quest for
certainty. Experience is his source of knowledge. He learns by
doing. Knowledge is the result and not the guide to action.
Whatever is found practical in achieving desired ends is good.
Religion is purely a private matter, consisting of individual beliefs
or aberrations which may hinder rather than help in building
the good life. In recent years there has been strong opposition
to the "progressive education" which Dewey fathered, because it
has produced a generation, not only ready to repudiate religion
and moral law, but to repudiate the American way of life. Many
churchmen viewed this God-denying philosophy as a direct attack
upon the Church, and they decided that if a climate favorable
to religion and morality could not be maintained in the public
schools, the time had come to withdraw their support from the
public schools and to establish schools of their own.

This estrangement between the churches and the public schools
has been intensified by the public school acceptance of the theory

of a "pluralistic society." This theory holds that America is composed of diverse religious groups and various elements without any religious convictions, and, therefore, it cannot any longer be considered either a Christian or religious nation. Organized minorities have mounted opposition to any semblance of Christian moral or religious influence still remaining in the public schools. Legal procedures are invoked to eliminate prayer and Bible reading, the appearance of clergymen in baccalaureate or commencement exercises, observances of Christmas and Easter, use of the Ten Commandments, and instruction in moral or religious values. Court decisions are usually favorable to the appellants on the ground of the religious pluralism of the community and the constitutional principle of separation of Church and State. Thus the secularistic forces in community life are encouraged to take complete control of the public schools. In some sections of the nation this erosion of church-school relations has made scant progress, but objective observers believe that it is only a matter of time until the last vestiges of religion and religious influence will be eliminated from American public education.

In this situation the course of the Christian churches and Christian parents becomes increasingly clear. If the rising generation of American youth is to be morally and spiritually illiterate because of the default of secular education, then the Christian churches and Christian parents must provide a completely comprehensive program of education. The challenge is unmistakable.

Christian day schools are being established at a rapid rate in all parts of the nation. These schools are of two types — community and parochial. The former are undenominational, nonsectarian, and controlled by Christian parents. These schools are committed in their charters to a statement of Christian doctrine and to a Christian philosophy of education. The parochial schools are owned and controlled by local churches and conducted as an integral part of their total educational program.

The Christian day school has the advantage of presenting a completely integrated Christian world and life view at every level of the educational process. There is no compromise with secularism, no heterogeneous conflict of educational viewpoints, no shifting perspectives. The student is spared unreconcilable outlooks and inconsistent interpretations respecting the whole of life in an educational world which has lost its way morally and spiritually. Instead of the Church's hit-and-run attacks on the secularism, materialism and humanism which confuse pliable minds and keep them wavering in a valley of indecision, there is a logically premised and developed educational philosophy coupled with a consistent curriculum and a reasonable and satisfying program. Communism presents this type of program with a carefully co-ordinated interpretation of the whole of reality from its naturalistic point of view. Our American educational muddle is no match for it. The Christian day school comes into this situation and offers a spiritual and moral leadership which is the only effective alternative to Communism and which can guide a wavering society into certainty and constructive achievement.

The Christian day school disposes of the popular cliché that religion embraces only one facet of life, and that one of inconsiderable pragmatic value. It exposes the error that the public schools can teach only science and the arts, which equip the pupil for practical citizenship, and the church can supply the moral or spiritual gap in his eduation in an hour a week in a Sunday-school class. Under such a system religion is likely to become an appendage, unrelated to the main stream of life. Christians believe that the Christian religion is basic to all of life and embraces every area of thought and action. Without Christ man is dead in trespasses and sins and 'unable properly to relate himself to God and to society. Christian education is the only education which can provide the pupil with a harmonious relationship to God and His immutable laws and give him the incentives and the spiritual power to live the good life individually and socially.

This idea of Christian permeation of all life and knowledge demands a Christian orientation of every subject taught in a Christian school. Science will be taught as truth, but scientific truth will be viewed as an integral part of all truth, which has its source in God. This gives scientific truth a deeper significance and causes the pupil reverently to exclaim, as did Newton when he discovered the law of gravity, "I thank thee, God, that I can think thy thoughts over after Thee." He can pray for guidance in research and be conscious of the help of God in making discoveries which are for the greater welfare of mankind. True piety and true learning go hand in hand. Truth in the perspective of Christian education has new meaning, new purpose and new uses.

It is often said that the existence of Christian schools tends to fragment our national society. This is not necessarily true, since Christian schools may also be American schools. They teach the patriotic principle of "the nation under God," conform to minimal national educational standards and co-operate in many community enterprises. They assume no pharisaical superiority or bigoted snobbishness toward non-Christians in public affairs. Christian education can make a tremendous contribution in building again the foundations which have undergirded American institutions and inculcating those moral and religious principles which have made America great. Without these foundations and principles democracy will wither and die. Christian education also offers a training ground for moral leadership in a time of ideological confusion and national weakness and indecision.

Organized Christian education should be a help rather than a hindrance to the cause of public education. Christian schools can challenge the public schools to do a better educational job. If the public schools have a monopoly on education they tend to become wearisomely homogeneous and non-progressive. Competition has always supplied the spice in American life and might well create a friendly educational interaction that would be beneficial to total American life. If the two types of education have a common concern for truth, time and judgment will eventually eliminate error and there will be increasing areas in which co-operation will be possible. In communities which are favorable to religion, Christian citizens should use their influence to elect capable and confirmed Christians to the boards of education and to encourage the selection of Christian teachers and administrators.

Christian citizens should commend every move on the part of the public schools toward the maintenance of moral and spiritual standards. On the other hand, they should make calm protest, intelligently and legally, against infringement of the moral and religious standards of the community. Where secularist and antitheistic teaching, and immoral social conditions are known to exist, the public should be informed and steps should be taken to correct the situation.

There are exceptional cases where American public schools are functioning much as they did in the "Mann Era" with respect to morality and religion. They still recognize the sovereignty of God in national life and honor the Judeo-Christian moral code. Particularly in the South and Midwest there are many rural and suburban schools which are controlled by Christian boards of education and staffed with Christian teachers, all quite sensitive to the claims of morality and religion. Religious practices vary according to geographical location and community mores. In some places the Bible is still read and prayer is still offered publicly each day. In others there is a weekly chapel service for which attendance is voluntary. Religious-type baccalaureate and commencement exercises are held. Released-time religious education is encouraged in many communities, though classes meet outside public school buildings. A good word must be spoken about the thousands of sincere Christian teachers in the public schools whose lives are a rich testimony for Christ. But when all has been said that can be said in favor of the American public schools, the naked facts of moral and spiritual erosion drive objective observers to the conclusion that Christian influence in public education is at an all-time low and is doomed to eventual eradication.

There is no question as to the legal right to establish Christian day schools in America. One of our most cherished liberties is freedom of worship and the free expression of religious conviction. Christian parents have the legally recognized right to teach and train their children in their religious tenets without interference. This means the right to co-operate with other such-minded parents in providing educational institutions for that purpose. Churches have, from the beginnings of America, maintained their own schools. Today over six million children are studying in such schools with full government approval. While a double burden of taxes and fees must be borne by those who would establish and maintain Christian day schools, the moral and spiritual values in individual and social life make such sacrifice eminently worthwhile.

There is a growing imperative for the development of a widespread movement to establish Christian day schools. America is standing on the brink of world-wide catastrophe. We must realize that Christianity is the only effective answer to the forces responsible for that catastrophe. The Church itself is threatened with destruction. Secular, naturalistic and humanistic education must be repudiated; every movement for the destruction of the Christian way of life must be challenged and defeated. The most telling and effective blow that Christians can strike for Christ and the things we most surely believe is to support sacrificially the establishment of thousands of new Christian day schools in strategic areas all across America.

The problems involved in building new Christian day schools are many and varied. Basic to the effectiveness of such schools is a clear-cut philosophy and policy. Such schools must hold fast the fundamentals of the Christian faith. They must integrate the Holy Scriptures with every area of human knowledge, and beyond the reaches of human wisdom seek to apprehend the things of the Spirit of God. They must preserve the freedom of thought and action providentially given the American people. They must provide every facility for scientific study in the realm of natural law. They must inspire youth to high attainment in whatever vocation of life they may serve God and humanity. Thus they will build men and women who will be good and faithful stewards of the talents which God has given them and who will grow into sterling citizens of the nation and the Kingdom of God.

The first requisite for the establishment of a Christian day school is not money or prestige, but Christian conviction and consecration. It has been done over and over again in almost every conceivable situation. What others have done can be done again. Local conditions will determine whether the undertaking should be sponsored by a local church on a parish plan, or by a group of Christian parents acting independently on a community plan. Those who truly love the Lord and see the imperative necessity for educational action should have no difficulty in agreeing on a minimal but sound doctrinal policy and a Christ-centered curriculum that meets high educational standards. Experienced Christian educators from nearby successful schools will be glad to give advice and guidance in the necessary legal, professional, organizational and fiscal steps which must be taken. As community opinion begins to crystalize, a public meeting should be called in which there can be a full discussion of the problems involved. A survey should be made to determine the potential enrollment for such a school. A Christian school society should be formed. From those who join, a small steering committee may be chosen to draft a constitution to be submitted to a subsequent meeting of the society for ratification. When this temporary committee has discharged its duties, a permanent School Board can be elected in accordance with the provisions of the constitution, and essential committees can be appointed. Usually the local pastor or pastors will take leadership in choosing teachers, providing temporary quarters for instructors, and promoting the best interests of the school in the churches and community. Where financial or other limitations require, such schools may begin with the first two grades the first year and grow, a grade a year, until a complete elementary, graded school, with courses meeting state requirements, has been established. In many communities there are often church educational facilities which can provide satisfactory temporary housing. In others, there are old public school or private school buildings which can be purchased and remodeled for use. Eventually every Christian day school should be housed in modern buildings, with equipment comparable to the best provided for public schools.

"Attempt great things for God; expect great things from God" and the resources of heaven will be poured out in great abundance.

Chapter XII

THE TIME IS SHORT

Knowing the time . . . now it is high time to awake out of sleep . . . (Romans 13:11).

I must work the works of him that sent me, while it is day: the night cometh, when no man can work (John 9:4).

THE Christian Church has always been at its best in times when it realized it was under a divine imperative for expeditious action. In such a climate sincere followers of Christ give themselves completely, sacrificially and in great faith for the accomplishment of high goals.

The night is far spent and the day of judgment is at hand for so-called Christian civilization.

The forces of Anti-Christ are sweeping the world. They are organized and equipped with weapons of destruction. They have a fully committed, well-indoctrinated and an absolutely determined leadership bent on world conquest. They are resorting to all sorts of stratagems, maneuvers, evasions, subterfuges and lawless methods to gain advantage.

The Church is gravely weakened by apostasy, worldliness, false pride, compromise and apathy, and it is in retreat.

There is danger of a nuclear destruction which could wipe out the human race in a matter of hours and plunge millions into a hopeless eternity.

The imminence of the Day of the Lord, which two thousand years ago impelled a few thousand Christians to unprecedented dynamic action and achievement, is two thousand years nearer at hand. Indeed, no man knows the day nor the hour when the Son of Man will come "as a thief in the night" to consummate His earthly ministry.

The time is short!

As never before in the history of the Christian Church and of the whole world, the divine imperatives of Christ for His followers have overwhelming meaning and significance. He is calling for unprecedented commitment and action.

The divine strategy for this crucial hour includes a new imperative in the field of Christian education. In this volume, an effort has been made to intimate something of that imperative. The time has come for the inauguration of a new movement for a vastly improved and expanded program of Christian education in every local church throughout the nation. This must be a "crash" program, not something to be mounted ten years from now or ten months from now, but NOW. *(Publishe d in 1967)*

There are already stirrings in the local churches. One church in a large American city was led to see the necessity for educational enlargement and advance. It began by calling a prayer meeting of a few consecrated workers. Then it moved with deliberate purpose to increase its weekly time schedule from one to two hours of instruction on Sunday, two hours on Saturday, four hours of additional supervised week-night home and church training. It co-ordinated the educational work of its men's and women's fellowships, youth groups, holiday retreats, camps and other semi-educational organizations in a well-ordered program, adding at least sixty hours more to the time schedule. It moved to open two grades of a new Christian day school, utilizing the splendid building and equipment which had lain idle during the week. If all Protestant churches would attempt half this ambitious program this year, they would be doing more than five times what the average Protestant church is doing in the field of Christian education.

Is it possible for every church to undertake such a revolutionary program? Undoubtedly. Small churches, it is true, cannot attempt as ambitious a program as the larger ones, but each according to its resources can DOUBLE what it is now doing.

How can this be done? The church mentioned above had a leadership of great faith and vision, which sensed the imperative necessity for a "crash program." The pastor, director of religious education and the department heads of the church school got together and prayed and decided to act. In their next meeting they received a report on their resources and the needs of the church and community, and a blueprint of educational advance which they accepted as well within their potential. Then these "counsellors" called a meeting of key teachers, leaders and workers and sold them the idea. The pastor then moved to bring this group into conference with the key church officials. They were so impressed with the unity, enthusiasm and faith of the church-school group that they approved the program. Soon a new church board of education was formed which put the program into action. All phases of church life which might be construed as educational were eventually integrated into a church-wide program. Heavy emphasis was laid on youth and adult education. A comprehensive and well-balanced curriculum was adopted. Assistant teachers were activated for full-time service. Special leadership training and teacher training classes were set up. A publicity and promotion committee, headed by a capable man knowledgeable in public relations, wheeled into action in both church and community. New pupils were recruited from both areas. In regard to enrollment the first responses were disappointing, but leaders rationalized and decided that those who responded represented progress and had faith to believe that this was only a beginning and that the Lord would reward their continued efforts. After the first quarter there was a noticeable increase and then the new program began to "snowball" until it became the "talk" of the whole community. The Christian day school was a sensation and brought the community up short in realization of its obligation to provide moral and spiritual instruction for its children and youth.

It is quite possible that there are many congregations which will never undertake such a daring and unconventional educational adventure. Their leaders will be so wedded to traditional programs and procedures that they will be unable to see the necessity for change and will be incapable of a faith willing to attempt the "impossible." But there are in these churches laymen who can be led to see the critical state of things and the imperative necessity of immediate action. They can pray and, if so convicted, seek the leadership of the Spirit in independent action. These people could well start classes in their own homes, enlisting neighbors and friends who would not be reached otherwise. Groups of likeminded persons could open Sunday schools in areas which are not being served by the organized churches. The blindness of religious leaders to their obligations, and to the potentials which exist in the laity, have been common to every age. Christ and His Apostles faced this situation in their day and leaders of every great reformatory movement in the history of the Church have faced it. It is well to remember that "God and one man can make a majority" in any righteous cause. Thousands of independent adventures of this type could bring great blessing to the Church and vastly expand the influence of Christianity in areas yet untouched by the Gospel.

Dr. Frank C. Laubach, the Christian missionary whose crusade for world literacy has accomplished wonders, says: "We are losing the war of education at a terrifying rate. Communists have captured a quarter of the world's people . . . by infiltration and indoctrination. It is late for us to save the world but not too late. . . . Our assets greatly outweigh our disadvantages. We have money. We have tremendous and highly capable man power. A new and better trained generation is coming on. There are a half million churches in America. If each one of these would double its educational program and would support a couple overseas to engage in educational evangelism we could far outstrip the Communists. . . . And let us not forget numbers of retired teachers and professional people who are primarily interested in educational work. They should be reactivated and assigned definite tasks. . . . It is late for us to save the world but it is not too late."

Today is the day for action. The time has passed for indecision. The Church must marshal all its resources. Christians must consecrate themselves anew to Christ. They must coolly, firmly and irrevocably resolve that He alone is their Lord and that they will serve Him only. His enemies must become our enemies and the enemies of our children; of our peace, our liberty and our happiness; of our virtue and our salvation. If we contend manfully against them and for the Lord, we will be more than conquerors in His name. The contest is fraught with hazard and alarm. Were it a war of arms, we would have little to dread, but it is a war of arts, of temptations, of enchantments, a war against "principalities and powers" and "wickedness in high places."

But fear not! In the words of Timothy Dwight, that great evangelical head of Yale University in the midst of a similar crisis in the life of the Church in America, "Almighty power will protect, infinite wisdom will guide, and unchangeable goodness will prosper you. The Christian world rises daily in prayer to heaven for your faithfulness and success; the host of sleeping saints calls to you from the grave and bids you Godspeed. · The spirits of your fathers lean from yonder skies to survey the conflict, and your children of many generations will rise up to call you blessed."